A Nightmare in History

A NIGHTMARE
IN HISTORY

The Holocaust 1933-1945

MIRIAM CHAIKIN

illustrated with photographs and prints

Clarion Books
New York

Frontispiece: Train tracks at Auschwitz today.

Clarion Books
a Houghton Mifflin Company imprint
215 Park Avenue South, New York, NY 10003
Printed in the USA
Library of Congress Cataloging-in-Publication Data
Chaikin, Miriam.
A nightmare in history.
Bibliography: p.
Includes index.
Summary: Traces the history of anti-Semitism from
biblical times through the twelve years of the Nazi era,
1933–1945 and describes Hitler's plans to annihilate
European Jews by focusing on the Warsaw Ghetto and the Auschwitz-Birkenau
concentration camps.
1. Holocaust, Jewish (1939–1945)—Juvenile literature.
[1. Holocaust, Jewish (1939–1945)] I. Title.
D810.J4C455   1987   940.53'15'03924   86-17617
PA ISBN 0-395-61579-8   ISBN 0-89919-461-3

HAL 10 9 8 7 6 5

זכור

In memory
of the three generations
who disappeared from Europe
1939–1945

Acknowledgments

For reading portions of the manuscript, thanks are due to Professor Louis H. Feldman, Rebecca Kook, Peggy Mann, Samuel Merlin, Professor Michael Meyer, Professor Robert M. Seltzer, Henry Tylbor, and Itka Frajman Zygmuntowicz. Special thanks to my editor, Ann Troy, for her abundant patience and guidance, and to Karen Peterfreund for editorial assistance.

Thanks also to Dr. Dennis B. Klein for reading and commenting on the book in manuscript form.

Photos: Most photos of the Holocaust period are copies of snapshots taken surreptitiously by Nazis, ghetto photographers, and unknown soldiers and civilians. The pictures were passed from hand to hand and copied. They therefore often lack the clarity found in professional photos. Where a photo appears in this book without a credit, the owner or source could not be traced.

Contents

Adolf Hitler is greeted by a cheering crowd in Godesberg,
Germany, 1938. *(UPI/Bettmann Newsphotos)*

Introduction

Adolf Hitler stood out in no way as a boy. He was an average student and finished high school without a diploma. As a young man, he tried to become an artist, but no art school would accept him. When he entered politics he seemed a comic figure — a lock of hair falling over his forehead, a square moustache, a public speaker who ranted and raved. Some people called him mad. Others laughed at him. They did not laugh for long.

Hitler was an evil genius. Qualities that had lain dormant in him began to surface. Fired by dreams of glory for Germany, preaching hatred, he formed the National Socialist German Workers' party — Nazis for short — and began a climb to power. Soon, when Hitler rode by, adoring Germans thronged the streets saluting him with an outstretched arm and calling, "Heil, Hitler!" — "Hail, Hitler!"

What drove Hitler? Two core aims. One was to win territory and power for Germany. The other was a set of racial beliefs. He spoke of people as races. In his view, Germans were pure-blooded and superior, a master race that deserved to rule the world. He hoped to improve the race further by making Germans perfect physical specimens, all with blue eyes and blond hair (though he himself was short and had brown hair and brown eyes). German cripples, the deformed and mentally ill, orphans and the homeless marred his image of a master race. He would deal with them when he came to power by destroying them.

In Hitler's scheme, other races were inferior. Especially Jews, Gypsies, Russians, Poles, and other Slavic people. They had mixed blood and were racially impure, and therefore worthless. The world did not need them. But one segment of this population could be made useful. He would destroy the educated classes, the leaders. And keep the masses as slaves. The million Gypsies in Europe were to be destroyed completely. A top Hitler aide made an exception among the Gypsies as well. He deemed two Gypsy groups to be racially pure. They were to be spared.

But no exceptions were to be made in the case of the Jews. Hitler had a pathological hatred of Jews. Though they had contributed much to the culture and welfare of Germany, he said they were parasites, a menace, polluters of the German race. For Jews, he had a special plan: *All* were to be destroyed. He would make the world, starting with Europe, *Judenrein* — a place without Jews.

In 1933, as soon as Hitler became *Der Fuehrer* — the leader — of Germany, he put his cherished beliefs into practice. His troops began a march across Europe, plunging the world into World War II. At the same time, he launched his racial plans. Nazi party members had sworn to follow him blindly. They were trained to be brutal and commit murder for the sake of the party's racial program. They brought fanatic devotion to the task of annihilating the Jews of Europe. With the same zeal with which police in other countries search for dangerous criminals, Nazis hunted for Jews.

The search was thorough. It included Jews who no longer practiced their religion, Jews who had converted to Christianity, even Christians who had only one Jewish grandparent. Rank-and-file Nazis conducted the searches. Their superiors were involved in planning and organizing. Nazi officers — doctors, lawyers, teachers — selected killing sites around Europe that would be suitable for mass murder. They arranged with German firms to provide systems that would destroy the greatest number of people in the shortest period of time, and at the least cost.

Hitler's fighting forces were the most powerful war machine the world had ever known. With his soldiers, tanks, and air force, he conquered almost all of Europe. In each country, his racial plans were activated. In each, Nazis hunted for Jews. He nearly succeeded in his aim of making Europe *Judenrein*.

Before the war, there were over nine million Jews living in Europe. The Nazis murdered some six million of them in cold blood. The Jews were not soldiers or wartime enemies. They were innocent civilians, men, women, and children whom the Nazis did not know and who had done the Nazis no harm. The three million Jews who remained alive were broken in body and spirit. Many died soon after the war. They had survived the war not because Hitler or the Nazis had a change of heart. They survived because Germany was defeated on the battlefield. Because the war had come to an end.

Only the Jews had been singled out for extinction. But they were not Hitler's only victims. The Nazis also savagely murdered over five million innocent Gypsies, Russians, Poles, Slavs, and others.

The twelve years in which Hitler was in power were a nightmare in history. Most western nations had lived by the values set forth in the Ten Commandments — love God, respect others, live with honor. Hitler turned the world inside out. On his march to power, he exported hatred and put opposite values into the air — cruelty, brutality, random murder. After the war the nightmare came to be called the *Holocaust*.

The destruction of a people was one side of the nightmare. The inhumanity of the destroyers was the other. Hitler was called mad. But the men around him were educated and cultivated. They were not mad. Germany was not a backward country but one of the most advanced nations in the world, renowned for great scientific and cultural achievements.

Because a civilized nation could commit such grotesque acts, and because a civilized world did not try to stop such actions, heads of state the world over agree that the nightmare must never be forgotten, that it must never be permitted to happen again. The philosopher George Santayana said long ago: "Whoever forgets the past is condemned to make the same mistakes in the future." Modern heads of state echo the thought. Former President Jimmy Carter, speaking in Washington, D.C. on International Holocaust Day in 1979, put it this way:

> Our words pale before the frightening spectacle of human evil unleashed upon the world. . . . But, we must strive to understand, we must teach the lessons of the Holocaust, and most of all we ourselves must remember.

Richard von Weizsaecker, president of West Germany, told the German parliament in 1985 that the Holocaust must not be allowed to fade from public memory.

The genocide against the Jews is without precedence in history . . . anyone who closes his eyes to the past is blind to the present. Whoever refuses to remember the inhumanity is prone to new risks of infection.

To keep the memory of the Holocaust alive for the sake of the future, every aspect of it has been documented — in books, diaries, films, trials, and the personal testimony of individuals, both Jews and Christians — who lived through it. There are libraries that house only Holocaust material. Yet some people — a handful — have begun to say that the Holocaust never happened. That the Jews made it up. Although their claim is generally regarded as twisted, it gives rise to a question. Have these people forgotten? Or don't they want to know?

The horrors of Nazi behavior defy belief. Even a willing memory is unable to hold the details for long. The passage of time also takes a toll. It dims such terms as *storm troops, death camps, roundups, gas chambers, crematoria.* The words resonate a time in history, and a place. But what do they mean?

The words represent key institutions that were the Nazi instruments of destruction. This book has been written to keep alive for memory's sake how the Nazi machinery annihilated six million Jews. And it traces the events that led to the nightmare that befell the Jews between the years 1933 and 1945.

The book opens with a short review of who the Jews are. And a review also of how anti-Semitism, prejudice against Jews, grew.

A seventeenth-century artist's rendition of Roman troops destroying Jerusalem in the year 70. (*New York Public Library Picture Collection*)

CHAPTER ONE

Anti-Semitism

The Noah story in the Bible tells how races started. Noah and his family were upright. The people around them were evil. God was angered by the evil. And God told Noah to build an ark and take aboard his wife, their three sons, and the sons' wives. Also two animals of every kind. When Noah and his family were safe in the ark, God sent a flood that drowned the other people.

Noah's sons, Ham, Japheth, and Shem, and their wives repopulated the world. From Ham and his wife came the people of Egypt and Ethiopia. From Japheth and his wife came the people of northern lands. Shem and his wife founded many people, including Jews and Arabs. Both are *Semites,* descendants of Shem. The term *anti-Semitism* is used only in relation to Jews.

Abraham was a descendant of Shem. Abraham and his wife Sarah were the first people to worship God. They came from Ur, in what is today Iraq. The people around them were pagans — they worshipped idols. God told Abraham to go to Canaan, on the other side of the Euphrates River, and found a nation that was devoted to God. He did so. Abraham was a rich donkey merchant. He and Sarah took their servants, flocks, and donkeys and journeyed to Canaan. There they founded the Hebrew people. The word *Hebrew* may come from the ancient word *iberu,* which means "donkey merchant." Or from *ibhri,* which means "one who is from across (the river)."

Jacob was the grandson of Abraham and Sarah. One night as Jacob lay sleeping, a stranger came and wrestled with him. The stranger was an angel of God. The angel changed Jacob's name to Israel, which in Hebrew means struggling with God. Jacob-Israel had twelve sons. Each headed a tribe that bore his name. The Hebrews were now called Israelites.

Over the centuries, the Israelites became a great nation. They lived by the Ten Commandments and other laws of justice and ethics that Moses, their prophet, had taught their ancestors. They had great kingdoms under kings David and Solomon. Jerusalem was their capital and the Temple there was the center of their lives. The Israelites daily offered animal sacrifices to God in the courtyard of the Temple. Animal sacrifice was the ancient form of worship.

Time, wars, and regional conflicts reduced the kingdom of the Israelites to the southern part of the land, around Jerusalem. The southern kingdom was called Judah, after the tribe of that name. The word *Jew* comes from Judah. The Jews continued to be the sole worshippers of God in the region. And to offer animal sacrifices up to God in the courtyard of the Temple. Then great world powers arose. First Greece, then Rome conquered Judah. The conquerors called the land Judea.

Under Rome, the Jews were free to practice their religion.

But they were no longer independent, no longer masters in their own land. They were ruled by Roman governors. The streets of Jerusalem were patrolled by Roman soldiers. The Roman governors were often corrupt and cruel. They freely executed people whom they regarded as enemies of Rome by crucifixion — nailing an individual to a cross in public. Almost each day, some slave or foreigner or Jewish rebel from Galilee in the north—a center for rebels — was crucified.

The daily life of the Jews went on as usual at the Temple. Also around the Temple, in the marketplace, in the shops and stalls. Jewish farmers offered fruits and vegetables for sale, merchants sold their fabrics, spices, jewelry, and other wares. Moneylenders, the bankers of that day, lent money for a fee. Dealers in sacrificial animals — sheep and doves — sold animals to the Jews who came daily to the Temple to offer up sacrifices.

In the first century B.C., there were three main groups of Jewish religious leaders. Sadducees, members of the wealthy class, performed the sacrifice ceremony. They believed in a strict interpretation of the Torah — the Law (the first five books of the Bible). Essenes, another group, lived in the desert, apart from people, and studied. Pharisees, the third group, were the teachers and preachers. They came from all classes of society and believed that the Torah was open to interpretation. Hillel, a leading Pharisee of the time, said all the laws in the Torah could be summed up in one phrase: Do not do to others what you would not want them to do to you. A Pharisee teacher was called *rabbi*, a Hebrew word that means "my master" or "teacher." Some rabbis taught in academies. Others taught in synagogues. Preachers were also often called rabbis. Some preached in synagogues, some on the Temple steps, others in the streets.

Yehoshua of Nazareth, a city in the Galilee, was a Jewish preacher. His name in Hebrew means "help comes from God."

The name Yehoshua is Joshua in English and Jesus in Greek. Jesus had a group of Jewish followers. From among them he chose twelve disciples whom he called apostles. He preached in the streets and byways, gathering crowds and urging people to live simply, to help the poor, and to feel compassion for the less fortunate. He was critical of the moneylenders at the market, who were charging excessive interest. Other rabbis and preachers also spoke out against unfair practices. But Jesus went further. He overturned the stalls of the moneylenders one day. Jesus stood out in other ways as well. His followers said he was divine and the son of God. They said he was the messiah — one who had been sent by God. They called him *Christ,* a Greek word that means "messiah."

Such claims were contrary to Jewish belief. In Jewish thinking, only God was divine. God was mysterious, invisible, and possessed no known shape. The nature of God was such that God could not father a son. At the time, talk about the coming of a messiah was common. There was conflict and tension in the land. Jews had lost their independence to the Romans. Their religious independence was also threatened. Rome was appointing unqualified Jews to be high priests. Jews hoped a messiah would come. They were waiting for a messiah to be sent by God, someone who would make people good and put the world right again. But they did not believe that Jesus was the messiah.

And the Romans in Judea? What did they think? They found the argument foolish. They saw nothing wrong with the world as it was, with the Roman world. They did not believe in messiahs. And they did not believe in the God of the Jews, who was not only one, a single God, but also invisible. They worshipped many powerful gods, chief among them Jupiter and Juno, who was Jupiter's sister and wife.

The religious argument did not interest the Romans. But the person of Jesus did. Roman rule was based on law and order. And the Romans saw Jesus as one of the rabble-rousers from Galilee. He stirred up the people and created disturbances. Also, he had taken the law into his own hands when he overturned the stalls of the moneylenders. In addition, his followers were growing. The small group of Jews around him had increased to a hundred. And they were calling him king. That would have been treasonous if it were not laughable. Rome ruled the world. Rome decided who was — and was no longer — king. The Roman governor of Judea at the time was Pontius Pilate, a harsh man. He was later recalled by Rome for the brutal means he used to suppress a local people.

These events are recounted fully in the part of the Christian Bible called the New Testament. The New Testament consists of four books about Jesus, and other writings. The four books are called Gospels, which means "good news." The Gospels offer this account of Jesus' death: A Jewish court met at night to try Jesus. They accused him of blasphemy for claiming to be the son of God. They found him guilty and turned him over to Pontius Pilate for execution. Pilate had no wish to execute Jesus. But, to pacify the court, he gave the order for Jesus to be crucified in A.D. 29.

Jewish historians view the circumstances of Jesus' death differently. Their reasons take into account what was happening in Rome and Judea around that time.

All of Jesus' followers were Judean Jews. They were called Jewish Christians. After Jesus' death, some of them went to

Rome to spread the message about Jesus and to gather followers. There was a second group of Jews in Rome, traditional Jews who were not followers of Jesus. The traditional Jews were given freedom to practice their religion and other rights. But Rome was hostile to Jewish Christians and savagely persecuted them. During the reign of Nero, in the year 64, they were thrown to dogs, to be torn to death.

At the same time, Judea was in turmoil. Roman governors oppressed the Jews. In the year 70, after many years of conflict and resentment, the Jews revolted. In a full-scale war that lasted three years, Roman soldiers killed over a million Jews, destroyed the Temple, and razed Jerusalem to the ground. Rome banished Jews from Jerusalem and forbade them ever to return.

The Gospels were written around this time — between about A.D. 70 and 100 — some forty to seventy years after the death of Jesus.

The historians believe that the Roman attitude toward Jewish Christians caused the authors of the Gospels to write as they did. They say the writers feared Rome and had to portray Jews in a bad light and Pontius Pilate in a good light.

Jewish historians make these additional points: The Jewish court in Jerusalem never met at night. They therefore question whether it ever met at all to put Jesus on trial. They say Jewish leaders had nothing to fear from Jesus. He posed no threat to the Jewish religion. Jesus was an observant Jew and taught the values of Jewish law. The Gospels quote him as saying this. Jesus did not seek to create a new religion but sought, as rabbis over the centuries have sought, to liberalize certain Jewish laws. Over a million Jews lived in Palestine. Jesus had between 200 and 250 Jewish followers when he died.

That situation would change greatly in due course. One thousand years of Jewish independence had ended. Some Jews remained behind in Judea after the destruction of Jerusalem. Many Jews went to Rome and other countries of the Roman Empire to live. The two sets of Jews living in Rome continued to hold different beliefs. But they also had much in common. Both worshipped God. Both prayed in synagogues. Both used similar prayers. Both observed Saturday as the Sabbath. Both celebrated Passover. They visited each other's synagogues, listened to each other's speakers, and argued about who was right.

Once the Jewish Christians began to admit pagans — Greeks, Romans, and others — into their circle of believers, the Jews began to be outnumbered. Soon all followers were simply called Christians. In the fourth century A.D., Constantine the Great, emperor of Rome, legalized Christianity and made it the official religion of the Roman Empire. And the Roman Catholic church was born.

The Roman Empire encompassed many lands and many people. The new religion needed to be shaped and organized for the millions of new Christians. And the church leaders set out to do so. Their first task was to remove the similarities between Christianity and Judaism, and divide the two faiths. They called the Bible of the Jews the Old Testament and the Gospels the New Testament. They said Christians had replaced Jews in God's favor. And that Christians were the true Israel. And they made rules: Christians were not allowed to marry Jews. They could not visit Jewish synagogues. Conversion to Judaism was punishable by death. The Sabbath was now Sunday, not Saturday. The holiday of Passover was replaced by Easter.

Some Christian leaders did not think the rules went far

enough. They thought the Jews should be punished for not accepting Jesus as the Messiah, or Son of God. They said Jesus had been killed by his own people, the Jews. (Although the Jews had no power to do so; only a Roman governor could order an execution.) And that all Jews should be held responsible for the act forever. They suggested that the church teach contempt — hatred — for the Jews. And that Jews be kept in a degraded state until they accepted Jesus as the son of God.

As a degrading device, Jews were required to mark themselves, to wear a badge of shame. The badge varied from country to country and period to period. In some places, Jews were made to wear yellow badges. In others, they were made to wear a particular kind of hat. Or clothing of a certain color or a certain cut.

Jews were barred from schools of higher learning. They were expelled from certain professions and forced into other professions, such as moneylending. In some places, they were forced on pain of death to convert to Christianity. In other places, they were forced to live in certain designated neighborhoods — in ghettos. From time to time, they were forced to leave one country or another.

Even without these rules, the Jews were vulnerable. They had lost their own country and were stateless. A Greek living outside of his country could turn to Greece for protection in time of trouble. And Egyptian could turn to Egypt. The Jews could turn to no one. They were a tiny minority in a Christian world. Their ways were different. And they stood out.

They rested on Saturday, their Sabbath. They went not to church but to a synagogue to pray. They prayed in a foreign language — Hebrew, the language of their ancestors. And woven into their prayers were words of love for their former

This fifteenth-century German woodcut shows a group of Jews in
the hats they were required to wear. *(New York Public Library
Picture Collection)*

capital, Jerusalem. They celebrated different holidays. And ate different meals, because their laws forbade them to eat certain foods. Their ordinary speech was different. They praised God frequently. If they made a plan, they acknowledged their dependency on God, adding the words *May it be the will of the Holy One, blessed be He.*

Many people have a natural dislike of strangers. They fear them. There is a word for it: *xenophobia.* This human response was not new to Jews. Their ancient history spoke of two episodes in which Jews were victims of xenophobia. In the earlier one, their ancestors lived in Egypt and the Egyptian pharaoh made slaves of them. The full story is recounted in the Bible in the book of Exodus. The second episode occurred later in Persia (Iran today). Haman, the grand vizier, or prime minister, of the Persian king, plotted to kill the Jews, but did not succeed. The full biblical story appears in the book of Esther.

The Jews now found themselves doubly vulnerable. They were not only strangers and different, and under suspicion for that reason. They were also blamed for the death of Jesus.

The church did not teach bodily harm. But an atmosphere of dislike and hostility had been sown, and attacks against Jews became almost inevitable.

Most people in Europe in the Middle Ages (about A.D. 500 to 1500) were ignorant. They were superstitious and ready to believe strange stories. And to spread them. They said Jews were devil worshippers. That Jews poisoned wells to kill Christians. That the Jewish religion obliged Jews to drink the blood of a Christian child on a Jewish holiday—a child they had, presumably, first killed for the purpose. Excited mobs periodically fell on the nearest community of Jews and murdered them. Local priests did not interfere. Popes and archbishops over the ages tried to put a stop to the killings. They sent word to local priests that Jews were not guilty of murder because Jews were not allowed to mistreat anyone, not even a dead body. But their words fell on deaf ears. Attacks against Jews continued. Sometimes the motivating factor was simple greed.

For more than a thousand years, the Catholic church was the only Christian church. This changed in the sixteenth century. Martin Luther was a Catholic priest in Germany. The pope was as powerful as a king. He was regarded as the final authority in matters of religion. Luther objected to this. He said the pope was a man, and that men make mistakes. In his opinion, priests also had too much power. Luther fought to remove these elements from Christian belief. His protests led to the formation of a separate branch of Christianity, the Protestant church.

Luther's reforms included a provision for Jews as well. He sought to change Christian attitudes toward Jews. In a booklet called "That Jesus Christ was Born a Jew," he said Jews were blood relatives of Jesus and "actually nearer to Christ than we are." He hoped that if Christian thinking were liberalized, Jews would convert to Christianity. But this failed to happen, and Luther became bitter and hostile to the Jews. Age and illness aggravated his outlook. In 1543, three years before he died, he wrote an article called "Concerning the Jews and Their Lies." In it, he recommended: "First, their synagogues or churches should be set on fire. . . . Secondly, their homes should likewise be broken down and destroyed."

Luther's reforms served to liberalize the church. But the position of the Jews was unchanged. Periodically, in this country or that, Jews were attacked in Protestant circles as well. Ignorant mobs attacked with fists and guns. Ministers

This wood engraving depicts a riot against the Jews at Frankfurt-am-Main, Germany, in 1612. *(The Jewish Theological Seminary of America)*

attacked from the pulpit. Writers attacked in books and pamphlets.

In 1789, a revolution took place in France that convulsed the world. The motto of the revolution was Liberty, Equality, Fraternity. These were new concepts. All along, kings and princes had ruled. No longer was this so. A new form of government came into being, one in which the people had a say — democracy. Such new concepts and ideas traveled across the borders of France. All of Europe began to change.

Jews also benefited from the changes. Most had been forbidden to own land. They had been barred from many professions. Higher education had been closed to them. Now they, too, could seek to broaden and improve their lives. Welcome as this liberalization was, the benefits had a dark side.

Some members of the upper classes, the traditional rulers, resented the changes. They thought power and privilege should remain in their hands. They opposed the spread of liberty and equality. All sorts of people were rushing to universities to study medicine, law, and other professions, adding unwelcome numbers to the educated class. The introduction of modern machines in factories was also creating a new class of society, a working class. The upper classes were losing ground, they were threatened. Others also felt threatened.

The ruling class would have liked to overturn, or at least slow down, these changes. How? For one thing, they could take the public's attention away from itself — by upsetting the people and rallying them around some central issue. Politicians began to throw dust into the public's eyes. Jews were the dust. They belonged nowhere and had no government to protect them. They had been persecuted for centuries. The public seemed willing to believe any wrongdoing on their part. Jews were an easy target. They began to be attacked for new reasons.

Claims that Jews poisoned wells or drank the blood of Christian children remained alive in the countryside, to erupt now and then. The new claims came from cities and places of power. Jews were accused in pamphlets and books for political reasons. The reasons varied. Sometimes they were in conflict. Jews were charged with being enemies of France.

They were also blamed for the opposite reason, for having been behind the French Revolution. In one pamphlet, they were accused of trying to take over the world. The pamphlet, a known forgery, became the bible of anti-Semites all over the world, and is in circulation to this day. It was pieced together from several sources, among them the following.

In 1807, a French writer, Abbé Barruel, wrote a book called *In the Service of the History of Jacobinism*. It was about a plot by a secret society to overturn the governments of Europe and take over the world. The book contained no mention of Jews. But some French anti-Semites thought it could be more useful if that connection could be made. A letter believed to be written by the French political police said that such a conspiracy did exist, and that the Jews were behind it. Book and letter were circulated together. They were translated into German, Russian, and other languages.

In Germany, in the 1860s, Sir John Retcliffe wrote a novel called *To Sedan*. One chapter dealt with twelve Jewish elders who gather at the cemetery at midnight to consult with the devil about their plans to take over the world. Anti-Semites saw the book as potentially useful. But it was fiction, a story, and had limited use as such. The book was rewritten to give it the appearance of fact. The twelve elders were replaced by a rabbi. The rabbi spoke not at a cemetery, but before a secret society of Jews. The subject? Their intention to take over the world. The rewritten work became *The Rabbi's Speech*. It appeared in the Russian press and was translated into other languages.

A French book, *Dialogues in Hell,* by Maurice Joly, also figured in the final document. The Joly book had nothing to do with Jews. But it was an argument about political power and how governments function. As such, it contained many rich ideas and useful points.

From these various works it appears the secret police of Czar Nicholas II (reigned 1894–1917) of Russia concocted the pamphlet. The powerful secret police were a major part of the Russian government. The czar was the last absolute ruler in Europe. Other absolute monarchs had passed from the scene. They had been replaced by parliaments and other elected governments.

Russia also trembled on the brink of change. Masses of peasants, who had been little more than slaves, had been given freedom — and with it a piece of land. The land was inadequate. Some peasants were worse off than before. Peasants were moving to the cities to find work in factories. Peasants and workers were demanding more rights and better conditions. There were strikes, riots, and shootings. The people were angry. Already, to avoid riots, the czar had been forced to make some reforms. The people wanted still more.

To direct the attention of the public away from the czar, the secret police circulated their pamphlet, which they called *Protocols of the Wise Men — or Elders — of Zion.* A protocol is an official document that lists points agreed to at a meeting. The police claimed the document was the secret minutes of a secret society of Jews.

The *Protocols,* repeating ideas from the Joly book, spelled out in great detail a plan to destroy Russia and Russian Christianity, and to take over Russia and then Europe and the world. And whose help would the Jews have in the massive undertaking? The devil's — an idea borrowed from the Retcliffe book.

According to one historian, when Czar Nicholas realized that the *Protocols* document was a fraud, he wrote on his copy, "We must not fight for a pure cause with unclean weapons." Nevertheless, the document was printed in the press. It "proved" to the reading public that Jews were seeking reforms in Russia not for the sake of the Russian worker, but in order to overthrow the czar and take over the government, and the world. The secret police used the document to organize *pogroms* — attacks — against the Jews. In 1881 and 1882, they further fired up peasants with such slogans as "Kill the revolutionists and the Jews." And "Kill the Jews and save Russia and the czar." In 1903, in Kishinev, they organized a major massacre during the Jewish holiday of Passover. Russian mobs savagely murdered fifty Jews, beat and mutilated hundreds, and looted some fifteen hundred Jewish homes and stores.

Despite the efforts of the Russian government to throw dust into the eyes of the Russian public, the people continued to clamor for rights, to strike, and to riot. And the first Russian Revolution broke out in 1905.

The *Protocols* did not disappear. They grew in importance. Russian politicians used the document to inflame the public throughout the Russian Revolution of 1917 and the bitter civil wars that followed.

Anti-Semites collected material that cast Jews in a bad light. They circulated such material and translated it into their own language. The *Protocols* were translated into German. In Germany, the leading anti-Semite of the day was Hitler. His political program was based in large part on anti-Semitism. He not only used the *Protocols* as "proof" of Jewish evil. He based some of his own political plans on its contents. Until then, anti-Semitism had been based largely on religious and political reasons. Now it was made a matter of race. This idea had been introduced earlier by other German anti-Semites. Hitler popularized it.

CHAPTER TWO

Hitler's Brand of Anti-Semitism

It appears that Adolf Hitler knew that the *Protocols* was a fake. But he found the document useful. It supported his views. The document showed Jews to be enemies of Germany, to be conspirators, to want to take over Germany. Hitler went one step further, emphasizing these qualities were in the blood of the Jews and were therefore a permanent feature of that race. Later, the *Protocols* would be introduced into German schools and used as a learning text. But at the beginning of Hitler's rise to power, he used the document to stir up his followers, a group of unemployed and disgruntled ex-soldiers like himself.

Hitler, ordinary as he seemed, turned out to be a mesmerizing public speaker. In the 1920s, he was the main speaker of the National Socialist German Workers' party. Nazis, its members were called for short. And the party program was based on Hitler's racial views. Hitler's speeches began to attract ever-larger audiences, and the party grew. Doctors, lawyers, teachers, and other members of the upper classes also began to join the Nazi party. Hitler could take credit for the growth of the party. He could, and did, and set himself up as its leader.

What was it he told his audiences? The mood in Germany was grim. Germany had lost World War I. Unemployment was widespread. Inflation wiped out people's savings. The German public was depressed. Hitler told his audiences what they wanted to hear. Screaming, his voice charged with emotion, he spoke of acquiring territory and winning glory for Germany. He told the German people that they were not to blame for losing World War I, they had lost it because of outside enemies — the Jews. Again and again, he made the same points: Germans were a master race, fit to rule the world. Nazis were a force for good in the world, Jews a force for evil. German Jews were polluting the German race by marrying Germans. And the Jews had taken over Germany. (In fact, there were six hundred thousand German Jews, and they represented one percent of the German population.)

His book *Mein Kampf* (My Struggle), the bible of the Nazi party, sets forth his racial views:

> He [the Jew] stops at nothing, and in his vileness he becomes so gigantic that no one need be surprised if among our people the personification of the devil as the symbol of all evil assumes the living shape of the Jew. . . .
>
> . . . I am acting in accordance with the will of the Almighty Creator: by defending myself against the Jew, I am fighting for the work of the Lord.

Hitler used God's name when he spoke to the public, but he was an atheist — he did not believe in God. He was against Christianity—Catholicism, the faith he had been born into, and the Protestant faith as well. Albert Speer, Hitler's friend, later wrote in a book that Hitler thought Christianity was the wrong religion for Germany. Speer quoted Hitler as saying: "Why didn't we have the religion of the Japanese, who regard sacrifice to the fatherland as the highest good? The Mohammedan religion too would have been much more compatible to us than Christianity . . . with its weakness and flabbiness."

In fact, Hitler hoped to replace religion with a new order — one based on race.

"Races were not created equal," he boomed at his audiences.

"Germany must be the foundation of an Aryan [German] world order."

"It is our duty to arouse, to whip up, and to incite in our people the instinctive repugnance of the Jews."

He did rouse the people, by spreading hatred for Jews not only in his speeches, but through the Nazi party press as well. *The Storm Troopers*, identifying itself as "a German weekly for the fight of truth," was typical of Nazi party publications.

Hitler dressed up his creed with symbols of power. He put his early Nazi followers into brown-shirted uniforms and called them storm troops. The name inspired fear. So did the way they looked, and the sound of their boots. They were called SA, the initials of their name in German. Hitler also created a Nazi flag: a red banner with a black swastika on a white circle. He did not invent the swastika. It was an old symbol, often of good luck, of many people around the world, including American Indians. The Nazi salute, an outstretched arm, accompanied cries of *"Heil Hitler!"* or *"Sieg Heil!"* — "Hail to victory!"

With such impassioned cries, Hitler's storm troops left the

Hitler at a Nazi mass rally. *(Yad Vashem)*

meeting halls after he spoke. Fired by his words, they went out into the street singing, "When Jewish blood gushes from our knives, things will be better." They did not only sing. They looked for Jews to beat up. With bully bravado, between five and thirty storm troopers often attacked one person.

Didn't the German government try to put a stop to the brutality? It did. But it was helpless. By the time the police arrived at the scene, the storm troops had fled. Also, there was public sentiment to contend with. Hitler's followers were numerous. They were everywhere. Out of sentiment, or out of fear, the public hesitated to interfere with the storm troops.

Hitler also spoke to his audiences of going to war. Wearing a brown, belted uniform and boots, surrounded by thousands of Nazis similarly clad, he called for a war of revenge — against France, Russia, the United States, Wall Street— and the Jews.

"Grit your teeth and think revenge! Learn how to settle with the men who hurled you into the abyss!"

"We do not want the thing they [the Jews] call unity, which includes everything that is rotten; what we want is struggle; struggle against Jewish democracy, which is no more nor less than a machine for the elimination of genius."

With Nazi banners flying overhead, he thundered into the microphone, filling the stadium, and the radio waves, with his pronouncements. The day was coming, he said, "when the banner of our movement will fly over the Reichstag [Parliament], over the castle in Berlin, yes, over every German house."

He was not wrong. In 1932, the Nazi party was the second largest political party in Germany. In January 1933, Hitler, former political unknown, was appointed chancellor — prime minister — of Germany. A year later, the German cabinet combined the offices of president and chancellor and made Hitler *Der Fuehrer* — the supreme leader, the unlimited master, of Germany.

The members of the armed forces swore allegiance not to the nation, nor to the principles of the nation, but to an individual, to Hitler:

> I swear by God this sacred oath, that I will render unconditional obedience to Adolf Hitler, the Fuehrer of the German Reich and people, Supreme Commander of the Armed Forces, and will be ready as a brave soldier to risk my life at any time for this oath.

As soon as Hitler took power, he put his beliefs into practice. First, he abolished freedom of speech and assembly, banned all parties except the Nazi Party, and had his political enemies murdered.

The Nazi party now reigned supreme. Party members had sworn to follow Hitler blindly — to protect him and his racial principles. And from the ranks of these loyal members, Hitler created an all-Nazi government dedicated to his racial beliefs. Besides the normal government agencies that control such functions as transportaion, agriculture, and banking, Hitler's all-Nazi government was made up of various agencies that controlled the public with tyranny. It had the power to arrest, condemn, and murder. Each of its agencies was headed by a close associate of Hitler. Each was dedicated to Hitler's aim to make Germany *Judenrein* — free of Jews — and to get Jews to leave voluntarily. The Nazi agencies launched a campaign to drive out the Jews. One of the means they used was terror.

The main agencies of the all-Nazi government were these:

Hermann Goering, Hitler's second-in-command, ran the Gestapo, the dreaded secret police. They murdered Hitler's political enemies, including seventy-seven Nazis whose loyalty Hitler questioned. They spied on the public, and arrested, tortured, and murdered people. The Gestapo had power over the courts. If a court found an individual not guilty, the Gestapo could arrest and imprison the individual.

Joseph Goebbels, in charge of propaganda, controlled all media — newspapers, magazines, movies, radio stations, and theaters. And he used all media to spread hatred of the Jews.

The black-shirted *Schutzstaffel* — security squad — was made up of several units. Its initials were SS. The SS were the elite of the Nazi party — doctors, professors, lawyers, and members of other professions — chosen for leadership qualities and a devotion to Hitler. They were trained to be cruel and ruthless. SS guards wore on their uniforms the death head emblem — a skull and crossbones — to signify that they were, as the symbol suggested, as obedient as corpses.

SS duties often overlapped those of the Gestapo. The SS conducted door-to-door searches looking for Hitler's enemies. The list was a long one: Jews, Communists, Socialists, clergy, trade union members, people who listened to foreign radio stations, Jehovah's Witnesses, unfriendly writers, journalists, judges, lawyers, teachers, homosexuals, and foreigners. A person could be arrested for any offense or for no offense at all.

The SS had its own intelligence unit, whose initials were SD. The SD spied on the government, looking for traitors and enemies, and on the SS itself. The SS also had its own courts and its own army, the *Waffen*, which was a part of the regular German army. Heading the entire SS was Heinrich Himmler.

Himmler put Reinhard Heydrich in charge of the SD. Heydrich would soon play a central role in Hitler's plans for the Jews. So would Adolf Eichmann, whom Heydrich appointed to head a department of Jewish affairs.

The Nazi party continued to function as a political party, building a membership for the future. It had branches in every neighborhood and on every block and searched for people who were not loyal to Hitler or his aims. It organized Germany's school children into Hitler Youth groups. The children, both boys and girls, wore swastika armbands and were taught to hate Jews. Children were encouraged to spy on their parents and other adults and to report anyone who

said anything against Hitler or the party. Nazi teachers told children it was all right to spit on Jews.

All non-Nazi voices in Germany were silenced. And the Nazis made wholesale arrests. They built new prisons for political prisoners, which they called concentration camps. The first was Dachau. This would soon become a dreaded name. People would be tortured there. They would disappear, never to be seen again. The second camp was Buchenwald. Other camps had been and were being built. Within a year, there would be fifty, located all over Germany.

Except for periodic lulls, the campaign of terror never ceased. Bands of storm troops and SS beat Jews in the street, raided synagogues, trod on sacred Jewish objects, and burned holy books, laughing and joking as they did so. They mocked, humiliated, and murdered Jews.

Goebbels fed the flames of hatred. All over Germany, the press reported false acts of Jewish treachery, stories about Jews drinking the blood of a Christian child, and other such lies. Movie houses, concert halls, cafés, and other public places put up signs reading Jews Not Wanted. Signs at swimming pools read No Jews or Dogs. In cabarets, German entertainers put on mock weddings between a German and a pig wearing a sign that said it was a Jew.

Hatred and suspicion were everywhere. Germans began to shun their Jewish neighbors and former friends and would not greet them in the street. German mobs felt free to loot Jewish stores and homes, and to attack Jews in the street. German children felt free to bully and beat their former Jewish friends and classmates.

Terror was one tactic Hitler used to get the Jews to leave. Many Jews belonged to the middle classes and owned stores. The SA and SS organized a nationwide boycott of Jewish stores.

Children were taught at an early age to support Hitler and his propaganda. (The Bettmann Archive)

(190) Blood-ritual accusations in *Der Stuermer*, April 1937.

An example of Nazi propaganda. The headline reads: RITUAL MURDER. The murder of ten-year-old Gertrude Lenhoff in Quierschied. Murderer: Jew. *(Yad Vashem)*

The memo from headquarters read:

The boycott will start on April 1 [1933]!
The boycott is not to begin piecemeal, but all at once; all preparations to this end are to be made immediately. Orders will go out to the SA [Storm Troops] and SS to post guards outside Jewish stores from the moment that the boycott comes into force, in order to warn the public against entering the premises. The start of the boycott will be made known with the aid of posters, through the press and by means of leaflets, etc. The boycott will start all at once at exactly 10:00 AM on Saturday, April 1. It will continue until the Party leadership orders its cancellation.

A Nazi guard posted in front of a Jewish store during the 1933 boycott wears a sign that reads: Germans! Beware! Don't Buy from the Jews! *(Yad Vashem)*

Goebbels drove around Berlin to see how the boycott was progressing. The scene that took place there was taking place all over the country. Armed, uniformed Nazis stood guard at every Jewish store and allowed no one to enter. Goebbels' diary entry for April 1 records his elation:

> All Jews' businesses are closed. SA men are posted outside their entrances. The public has everywhere proclaimed its solidarity. The discipline is exemplary. An imposing performance! . . . There is indescribable excitement in the air.

And what about the Jews? They were in a state of shock. Jews had been living in Germany for over a thousand years. They had thought of themselves as Germans. Jewish sons and brothers had been killed fighting in Germany's wars. Jews had contributed greatly to the cultural and industrial life of Germany. *Judische Rundschau,* a German-Jewish newspaper, early alerted its readers with a carefully worded warning:

> We live in a new period, the national revolution of the German people is a signal that indicates that the world of our previous concepts has collapsed. . . . The only survivors will be those who are able to look reality in the eye.

Jews who looked reality in the eye left, and continued to leave, Germany. Those who could afford it went to America and other distant places, out of Hitler's reach. A Jewish welfare agency, the American Joint Distribution Committee, helped others to get to Palestine (Israel today). So did Palestinian Jewish groups. And the Jews who remained behind? They could not believe that the madness would last. They were sure it would pass.

It did not. The situation worsened. Jewish men were taken away in droves to concentration camps and made to haul stones fourteen to sixteen hours a day. Those who lagged behind or complained were lashed to trees and beaten.

In 1935, Hitler made anti-Semitism German law. At his urging, the parliament, meeting in the city of Nuremberg on September 15, 1935, passed a series of laws that stripped Jews of citizenship. The laws expelled Jewish doctors, lawyers, teachers, musicians, writers, actors and others from their professions. They expelled Jewish children from school. Jews had to have their official papers stamped with the letter *J* for *Jude* — Jew. They also had to change their names. Men had to add *Israel* to their names, and women, *Sarah*.

So that all Germany would know who was subject to the laws, a law also made clear who was a Jew. In the Nazi view, Germans were Aryans, a pure-blooded race. The law said anyone who had one Jewish parent or was descended from even one Jewish grandparent had tainted blood and was to be considered non-Aryan.

Jews and Christians had been intermarrying for years. They had children and grandchildren. People who had thought of themselves as Christians suddenly found themselves listed as Jews. New segments of the German population found themselves in the grip of Nazi terror. Christians with a Jewish mother, father, or grandparent. Christians who were married to Jews, or whose children were. Jews who had not practiced their, or any religion, for years. They tried frantically to cover up the facts or to hide. But the Nazis conducted savage hunts for them, and found them.

Each fresh wave of anti-Jewish measures caused more Jews to flee. Among them was the Walter Jacobsen family. Their experience was typical. Their ancestors had lived in Germany for generations. Their little seven-year-old daughter, Ruth, had been expelled from school for being Jewish. Her parents had transferred her to a Jewish school so she could continue her education. Ruth came home one day and reported that the Nazis had burned down her school. A Dutch Christian friend who was visiting urged the family to leave at once for Holland, where they would be safe. They did so that same day, taking only the clothes they wore.

As far as the general German public was concerned, most considered Hitler as something of a savior. Some were literally taught to think that. The SS ran welfare programs. German children taking part in a free meal program in Cologne were taught a verse before a meal. The first two lines were:

> Fuehrer, my Fuehrer, bequeathed to me by the Lord
> Protect and preserve me as long as I live.

Economic conditions had improved throughout Germany and most people were grateful. Hitler had given jobs formerly held by Jews to other Germans. He had created additional jobs with public works programs. He had put former Jewish businesses and property into non-Jewish hands. He had enriched the German treasury by seizing Jewish property and bank accounts. Some Germans did not approve of Hitler's racial policies. Or of what he was doing to the Jews. They might have liked to protest, but they would only face arrest. Some might have liked to extend a helping hand to the Jews, but they were afraid. The Gestapo and SS had eyes and ears everywhere. Or their neighbors, perhaps even their own children in the Hitler Youth, might inform on them.

The terror campaign had paid off. Besides jobs and money gains, the *Judenrein* project was well under way. Half the

Jewish population had fled. Many Jews had committed suicide. The Nazis had murdered about one thousand and put tens of thousands into concentration camps. The thousands of Jews from East European countries living and working in Germany had been and were being deported. The Gestapo had rounded up eighteen thousand Polish Jews in the middle of the night, packed them onto waiting freight trains, and shipped them off across the border to Poland. The towns and villages of Germany were *Judenrein* — empty of Jews.

The only Jews left in Germany were in Berlin, the capital. They could not bring themselves to leave children or spouses behind. Or they were afraid to go to an unknown place. Or they had convinced themselves that the German people would soon topple the Hitler government. Or that the outside world was getting ready to put a stop to the Hitler regime.

The rest of Germany was *Judenrein*. In towns and villages where Jews had once lived no Jewish footsteps sounded. All signs of Jewish life were gone. Here and there, something indicated that Jews had once lived in a place. A cellar wall in Cologne, where Jews had been hiding, bore such a hint. Before being arrested, deported, or worse, someone had written on the wall:

> I believe in the sun even when it is not shining.
> I believe in love even when not feeling it.
> I believe in God even when God is silent.

CHAPTER THREE

The Goal Is Annihilation

Nor did Hitler ignore his promise for additional territory. On March 12, 1938, German troops marched into Austria. To Hitler's surprise, and that of the German high command, the troops met no resistance. They were welcomed with flowers.

With unbelievable ease, Hitler became master of Austria. His racial beliefs did not stop at Germany's borders. In Austria, too, he launched a campaign against leftist political groups and the Jews. The Nazis had developed many tactics in Germany for terrorizing Jews, humiliating them in public, spreading hatred against them.

The SS in Austria marked Jewish shops and ordered Austrians not to buy there. If they caught someone doing so, they made the person wear a sign around the neck saying, I, Aryan Swine, Have Bought in a Jewish Shop. On a Saturday, the Jewish Sabbath, the SS seized Jewish men in the street and took them to the park. They made the men get down on all fours and eat grass, then made them climb a tree and twitter like birds. Other times they made Jewish women, including pregnant women, run until they fainted. Whatever indignity they could devise, they visited on their victims. Humiliating Jews, making them objects of ridicule, would become standard Nazi practice throughout Europe.

Now that Austria was German territory, it too had to be made *Judenrein*. Adolf Eichmann came from Germany for the purpose. He rounded up Jews and began deporting them, some to concentration camps in Germany, others across the border to Czechoslovakia.

Unknown to the German public, Hitler and the German high command had earlier discussed plans to go to war. They were ready to make a move. But the mood in the country was not right. The people were not ready for all-out war. More to the point, neither was the army. An event was needed to shake up the public. Such an event presented itself.

Among the Polish Jews who had been expelled from Germany by the Gestapo and sent to Poland was the Gryznszpan family—Zindel, his wife, daughter, and a son. A second son, seventeen-year-old Herschel, was in Paris. When Zindel wrote Herschel telling him of the family's expulsion, Herschel became enraged. On November 7, 1938, the boy went to the German embassy in Paris and shot the first official he met. The boy was arrested. The official died on November 9.

The Nazis had the event they needed. It had been the act of an unbalanced boy. But they would proclaim that the shooting was part of a Jewish plot to destroy Germans. They did so. They organized demonstrations. The demonstrations were to appear spontaneous, as if the public, outraged by the actions of the Jews, had gone on a rampage.

On the night of November 9, Nazis wearing regular clothes and armed with hammers, axes, and grenades took to the streets crying, "Down with the Jews." They were

The window of this Jewish store was violently smashed on *Kristallnacht*, November, 1938. *(The Jewish Theological Seminary of America)*

joined by others. Before long there were angry mobs. And for the next twenty-four hours, all over Germany and Austria, brutal mobs roamed the streets, smashing the windows of Jewish stores, setting fire to or destroying synagogues, and demolishing and looting Jewish homes. The event was called *Kristallnacht*—Night of Broken Glass. Jews were made to pay for the damages. Some thirty thousand Jews were arrested and sent to concentration camps.

Germany—and Austria—were shaken by the episode. A

few months later, on March 13, 1939, Hitler invaded Czechoslovakia. The Jewish story was repeated—not for the last time. The SS moved their campaign of abuse and terror there. Jews had been living in Prague for a thousand years. Eichmann came to make Czechoslovakia *Judenrein*.

In the meantime, Germany was enjoying economic growth. More and more German factories were opening—in Germany and in the conquered territory. There were not enough workers to fill the jobs. Eichmann deported young, strong Czech Jews to concentration camps in Germany as "slaves." The others he deported to Poland.

The outside world had called Hitler "tyrant," "dictator," "despot." But no country had tried to stop him. On the heels of his successes, Hitler and the German high command struck again.

On September 1, 1939, the German army swept across Poland. England and France had treaties with Poland. They had to come to Poland's defense. Both declared war on Germany, and World War II commenced. Before the month was out, Poland had surrendered, and Germany was in control of that country as well. And the Nazis had a new—and very large—Jewish population to torment.

Poland was teeming with Jews. It contained not only the large native Polish-Jewish population. Additional thousands of Jews had fled from Germany, Austria, and Czechoslovakia, hoping to find safety in Poland. Incredibly, they found themselves once more trapped in the Nazi nightmare. Once more they had to flee. Everywhere, Jews streamed out of the cities and towns. The roads were clogged with refugees toting bundles and pushing carts laden with their movable belongings. Where were they going? They did not have much choice. They were heading for a town where the Germans had not yet arrived, or were not yet in full control.

In Poland, the Nazis used the same tactics they had perfected elsewhere and invented new ones as well. They made Jews wear a six-pointed star on their clothing and carry a Jewish identity card. Jews had to tip their hats to a German in the street and get off the sidewalk when a German passed. To amuse themselves, some Germans changed the regulation on the spot and beat a person who tipped his hat for not knowing that the regulation had been changed. They cut the beards of pious Jews and made Jewish men do push-ups on the sidewalk. They made Jewish men in a synagogue spit on their sacred objects, then shot the men. They shot entire groups of Jews. They seized Jewish men in the street and put them to work digging ditches and latrines, clearing snow and war rubble. They made young Jewish girls clean latrines with their hands. They put up signs in trolley cars reading Jews-Lice-Typhus and Whoever Helps a Jew Helps Satan.

Vladimir Jabotinsky was a well-known writer and prominent Jewish leader. Before Hitler invaded Poland, Jabotinsky traveled around Poland telling Jews that Hitler and the Nazis would not disappear any time soon. He urged the Jews to leave Poland and go to Palestine to save themselves. In 1938, he told the Jews of Warsaw at a public meeting:

> Whoever of you will escape from the catastrophe, he or she will live to see the exalted moment of a great Jewish wedding: the rebirth and rise of a Jewish state.

But, like the Jews of Germany, Austria, and Czechoslovakia, most Polish Jews could not bring themselves to leave, or were afraid to, or did not know where to go. Some had heeded Jabotinsky's warnings. Wolf Manheimer, a young

Polish Jews with their possessions in bundles moved from place to place in an effort to elude the Nazis. *(UPI/Bettmann Newsphotos)*

Polish boy, and a friend got on bicycles and began pedaling toward Palestine. The boys did not make it. Italy had a treaty with Germany. The boys got as far as Italy, where they were arrested and sent back to Poland. Others reached Palestine safely.

The war raged on. England and France continued to drop bombs on German targets. Germany's need for workers became and remained critical. The Nazis seized able-bodied Jewish men in the street, as if the men were no more than logs, and sent them away as slave laborers. This, too, would become standard Nazi practice.

A man who survived those years remembers walking down the street with his father in Warsaw. He was seven years old at the time. The Germans seized his father and led him away in handcuffs. The child was left standing on the street, terrified and sobbing. He never saw his father again.

The triumphant Germans saw victory as proof of Hitler's greatness and of his claim that Germans were a master race. But success, while welcome, presented Hitler with an unexpected problem—a Jewish problem. Hitler's dreams did not end with Poland. He dreamed of conquering all of Europe. And there were Jews everywhere. There were some three-and-a-half million in Poland alone. He could not arrest them all. Nor could he ship them elsewhere. With a large part of Europe already under his control—and more to come—there was no "elsewhere."

The situation required a different solution. And Hitler had one. He had been harboring a plan for some time. Hitler's new goal was *Vernichtung*—annihilation. The Jews were to be destroyed. *No Jew in Europe was to be left alive.* The goal was to be kept secret. Hitler was very firm about that. He swore his aides to secrecy. True, it was inevitable that the outside world would see pieces of the plan in operation. But it was agreed that some reasonable explanation could be invented as a cover-up. However, under no circumstances was anyone to learn of the goal.

Hitler's top aides kept the plan secret even among themselves. They spoke of it only in code. They called it the "final solution." They spoke of its parts also in code. The word *deportation* meant "round up and kill." Poland was east of Germany. *Evacuation to the east* meant "round up and kill in Poland." Reinhard Heydrich was in charge.

In Germany, in Berlin, two weeks after Germany took over

Poland, Heydrich met with heads of the *Einsatzgruppen*—special duty groups—under his command. The men understood what was expected of them when Heydrich spoke of the "final solution." They understood that Poland was to become a mass graveyard. They came to an agreement: the plan could not be accomplished overnight. It would take place over a period of time, and in stages. It was to begin at once.

Heydrich sent minutes of the meeting to the Nazi leadership. They began, after reaffirming the need for secrecy:

> The first step for the final aim [another code word] is the concentration of the Jews from the countryside into the large cities.

That was to be stage one of the plan. Choosing large cities was a practical measure. Most Jews already lived in them. Also, large cities were on or near railroad tracks. The Nazis would also soon begin building death camps on railroad tracks. That, however, was for stage two of the plan. For the time being, the SS in Poland began organizing ghettos and herding into them the three-and-a-half million Polish Jews.

Nor was the German army asleep at the time. In the spring of 1940, in a matter of days, German tanks rolled across Europe conquering Denmark, Holland, Belgium, and France. Everywhere, the SS came in to set up ghettos or concentration camps and put into motion stage one of the "final solution."

The Jacobsen family that had fled to Holland for safety when little Ruth's school was burned down? They were no longer safe. The Jewish story was repeated in all conquered countries, including Holland. Jews there were ordered to wear a star on their clothing. Little Ruth was again expelled from school. Again her parents sent her to a Jewish school. The Nazis were sending out letters, requiring all Jews to register. Ruth told her parents that the children at school who had registered had never come back to school again. They and their families had disappeared.

The Jacobsen family listened on the radio to Hitler's hysterical speeches screaming for *Ausradieren*—"erasing" the Jews from Europe. They did not go to register when the letter came. With the help of the Dutch underground, the family went into hiding. Ruth is a biblical name and common among Jews. For safety's sake, her name was changed to Truusje, a Dutch name. The underground placed her with a family in the north. The family called her their niece and said she had come to stay for a while.

Ruth's parents were hidden with a family in the same town, in the attic of a house. The parents had to remain very quiet. There were children living downstairs who might innocently blurt out the secret that people were hiding in the attic. It was better that the children not know. Once in a while, if there were no Nazis around, the underground brought Ruth—or Truusje—to her parents at night for a visit. She sat with them in their tiny, crowded room, not moving, speaking in whispers and playing cards.

Because Ruth had no identity card and could not be enrolled in a Dutch school, she roamed the streets all day. Children in the neighborhood grew suspicious of her. The Nazis were everywhere. Periodically, to keep people in a state of terror, they roped off a neighborhood block by block and went from house to house searching for Jews. When the underground learned that the Germans were planning to make a search of the block in which Ruth lived, they took her away and placed her with another family, this time in the south of Holland.

All over Europe it was the same. Jews were packing, fleeing, going into hiding, trying to get illegal documents—fake identity cards that said they were Christians—in order to escape. They fled by car, by truck, by horse and wagon, and by every means possible. Some had to walk from one country to another. The Szer family of France was among these.

Annette Szer Baslaw was a thirteen-year-old French girl when the Germans came. The Germans were rounding up Jews. She and her mother and father were forced to flee. They could not leave by train because the Nazis checked the papers of all travelers. The only escape was to cross the border to Spain secretly on foot. Borders were closely guarded by Nazi patrols. The only possibility was to hire a guide who knew out-of-the-way roads that were not watched. They would have to travel by night to escape detection. The Szer family gave all their money to Spanish guides to take them to Spain. The guides brought them up a mountain and disappeared in the night with the money. The Szer family was stranded and penniless. They did not know where they were or which way to turn. They began to walk, hoping they were not heading back to France. They walked all night and slept in the daytime, hiding not only from Germans but from peasants who might be tempted to turn them in. The Germans offered rewards of money for information about Jews. After some days, the three arrived by foot in Spain; eventually, they reached Portugal.

While this kind of frantic activity was going on in Jewish communities all over Europe, the SS in Poland was busy with stage one. At the same time plans were also underway for stage two. Other SS were looking for other methods suitable for mass killing. A bullet was limited in what it could do. It could kill only one person at a time.

The Nazis busy with stage one were organizing some fifty ghettos of various sizes all over Poland, marking off a part of the city, usually the slum, as the place that would be the Jewish ghetto section. There, they announced, and nowhere else, all Jews must live. Christians who had been living in that section were ordered to move out. And all Jews living elsewhere in the city—and those in the towns and villages nearby—were ordered to move in within twenty-four hours.

The ghettos bore no resemblance to the ethnic ghettos of today. They were prisons—surrounded by a wall and controlled by brutal, armed Nazis and their equally brutal non-German helpers. The Nazis found many willing helpers throughout Europe. The most numerous and energetic were volunteers from the Ukraine, a part of Russia, and from Lithuania, Latvia, and Estonia. They became helpers not only in their own countries but also in Poland. And not only in the ghettos but also in the death camps.

CHAPTER FOUR

The Warsaw Ghetto

Warsaw is the capital of Poland. Many Jews lived there. In November 1940, one year after Reinhard Heydrich's secret meeting in Berlin, the largest ghetto, the Warsaw ghetto, was established. (The Lodz ghetto was already in existence.) All ghettos were controlled by Nazis and their helper guards. All were run along the same lines. The story of the Warsaw ghetto is the story of all ghettos.

The Warsaw ghetto consisted of one hundred square city blocks of a slum section of the city. Around the ghetto, to enclose it, the Nazis had the Jews build a brick wall some eight feet high. Christians lived on the other side of the wall, free. Jews lived inside as prisoners. Guards with rifles and machine guns stood posted at the openings, ready to obey the law, which read:

> Jews who leave without authorization will be punished by death. The same punishment applies to persons who knowingly provide a hiding place for Jews.

Starving orphan children were a common sight in ghetto streets.
(Yad Vashem)

Once all Jews had been moved into the ghetto, close to four hundred thousand Jews were packed inside. Their normal lives had been yanked to a close. Parents no longer had safe homes to offer their children. Children no longer had a childhood. Most of the children in the ghetto were orphans, many under the age of fifteen. Their parents had been sent to labor camps or had been murdered. Or they had died in a bombing or of hunger or disease.

The SS officer in charge of the ghetto reported to his superior on the housing arrangements he had made for the Jews:

> There are about 27,000 apartments with an average number of two and a half rooms. Occupancy therefore works out at 15.1 persons per apartment and 6 to 7 persons per room.

About two or three families unknown to each other, some ten to twelve people, lived together in just two rooms, a kitchen and bathroom. Some people slept on the kitchen table, some under it. In winter there was little heat. Keeping clean and having enough water were problems throughout the year. Pipes and plumbing fixtures that broke down were never fixed again.

The ghetto had many features in common with any slum. The streets were dirty and crowded, the apartment houses run-down. Many stores stood empty, having been looted by German and Polish police. There were pharmacies, but they had no drugs to sell. Hospitals were not functioning. Private homes had been turned into hospitals. These, along with the old-age homes and the orphanages, were full to overflowing. There, the resemblance ended.

A Jewish mother and her children in the Warsaw ghetto. *(Yad Vashem)*

Signs of extreme poverty were everywhere. Most people walked about in rags. Hunger was the scourge of every ghetto. It was wartime, and food was scarce for everyone, inside and outside the ghetto. Food had to be rationed, only so much for each one. That did not mean the rationed foods were always available for purchase. Bakeries did not always have flour to bake with. Peddlars who sold bread from carts in the street did not always have bread to sell. Rations were set by the Germans. Germans received the most bread and potatoes. Poles received a lesser amount, but enough to live on. Jews received starvation rations.

The rations were deliberate. It was Nazi policy to kill as many Jews as possible by natural means. And one of the means was starvation. Many people died daily of starvation.

Also of typhus, spread by flea bites, and typhoid, caused by contaminated water and poor sewage systems. Corpses littered the streets. Undertakers went about with hand-drawn or horse-drawn carts, collecting corpses and taking them away for burial. Jews were in rags because they had to sell off whatever they owned, down to underwear, to have enough money to buy food. When they had nothing more to sell, they took to the streets with tin cups, begging.

Terror was used by the Nazis as an instrument to spread fear and keep order in the ghetto. Routinely, the Nazis clubbed men, women, and children, or kicked down people's doors in the middle of the night. They shot into the air to frighten people. More often they shot at live targets—some passing Jew or group of Jews. The shootings were not confined to the ghetto. The Nazis rounded up groups of Jews in the street, or seized them from their homes, took them to a nearby forest, a deserted village, or to the local cemetery, and shot them.

As for the day-to-day life of the ghetto, the Jews set up, by order of the Nazis, a Jewish Council. The council was not a free agent. It took orders from the Nazis. It dealt with housing, sanitation, food, schools for the children, and such. Also with the thousands of Jewish refugees the Germans were rounding up and bringing to the ghetto. The refugees swelled the population to over 450,000. They had been forced by the Nazis to leave with only the clothes they wore. Most arrived in rags, often without shoes—starving, dirty human wrecks. The ghetto had no housing for them, and no food rations either.

The council could offer them only unheated synagogues and other public buildings to sleep in . The street orphans also slept here, or in the doorways of apartment houses. And public soup kitchens were set up. But there were thousands of refugees and street orphans. The soup was not enough to go around. The refugees and the orphans took to the streets, begging for food or for money to buy food. Even the refugees who arrived better dressed and better fed were soon in rags and begging in the streets. The cries of hungry children were heard throughout the ghetto every night.

"These were not human cries, nor human weeping, but the haunted baying of creatures facing death," Dr. David Wdowinsky, a Polish psychiatrist, wrote after the war.

The only way to get enough food was to smuggle it in from the outside. The Christians living on the other side of

Children crying in the streets of the ghetto. *(Yad Vashem)*

the wall could count on at least one daily meal of black bread and potatoes, sometimes even a vegetable. Food could be bought there, but getting there was a problem. Jews were not allowed to leave the ghetto. Anyone caught smuggling in food was shot. The death penalty stopped no one. Ghetto life offered two choices: to die quickly of a bullet, or slowly of hunger.

The Jews built underground tunnels to the other side of the wall. And found sewers that led there. And located loose bricks in the wall that could be removed and put back again. And through these secret passages, or by climbing the wall —even though the Nazis made them add broken glass and barbed wire to the top of the wall to discourage escape— smugglers went out daily in search of food. Smuggling, normally an illegal activity, a wrongful act, was the only way the Jews could keep from dying. And day and night, smugglers stole out of the ghetto through one of the secret passages and returned the same way, with food to sell and to eat. Many children, because they were small and lithe, became successful smugglers. Adult smugglers were less successful, and were often caught and shot.

The Nazis also sought to destroy the spirit of the Jews. And the Jews used all means possible to combat this objective as well, and to keep up their morale. They had been forbidden to pray in synagogues. So they prayed in each other's houses and celebrated all Jewish holidays as fully as they were able. They even had parties on occasion, meeting behind drawn window shades, making speeches, telling jokes about the Nazis, and singing familiar songs.

They sang new songs as well. The songs came from the secret couriers who traveled from ghetto to ghetto. The couriers' task was not to bring songs. It was to bring news, information, or material things. But if a song had become popular, they passed it along. In the Bialystok ghetto, some five thousand Jews were shot by the Germans on a Saturday, the Jewish Sabbath. The widows of the men who were killed were called *shabbesdikkeh*—the Sabbath ones. Paysakh Kaplan, a poet in the ghetto, wrote a song in honor of the widows—"Rivkale the Sabbath One." Rivkale, a woman, does not know that her husband has been killed, only that he has been taken away. One stanza speaks of her wretchedness as she toils at her sewing maching in the ghetto factory where she works:

> Where is he, my darling one,
> Does he still live? Where?
> In the concentration camp
> —Is he slaving there?
> Oh how dreadful is his lot,
> How horrible is mine—
> Since that fateful Saturday,
> Since that day, that time.

Another song came from the Vilna ghetto, in Lithuania. Vilna had been a great Jewish cultural center, with many poets, writers, and learning academies. It was called "the Jerusalem of Lithuania." In Vilna, and all over Europe, the Nazis were taking children away and sending them no one knew where. Shmerke Kaczerginski, a Vilna poet, wrote a song called "The Lonely Child." The first stanza is:

> Something unknown now runs after me.
> My mother, dear mother, oh, where can you be?
> Your little Sarah is calling, little Sarah, your child . . .
> Whose cries cross the fields like a wind that howls wild.

Above all, for the sake of the children, the Jews of the Warsaw ghetto tried to make life seem as normal as possible. School teachers taught them regular subjects. Artists taught them art and musicians taught music. Women collected books from around the ghetto and established secret libraries for children. The children sang in choirs, attended plays, and put on plays. There were cultural programs for the adults as well. They went to lectures and concerts and also attended plays.

Isolation imposed by the Nazis was another factor the Jews had to struggle against. They were to have no contact with the outside world. The Nazis had confiscated their radios and forbidden them newspapers. However, there was both a radio in the ghetto and a secret newspaper. The men and women of the Jewish underground followed the war news on their secret radio and reported it in the underground paper. And their secret couriers moved in and out of the ghetto with news or documents.

The work of a courier was dangerous. A courier who was discovered was killed. The Germans controlled the country. They allowed no one to pass without checking his or her identity card. The underground provided couriers with Christian identity cards to assure a measure of safety. The identity cards were forgeries made by the underground. Sometimes a Christian identity card was real. The underground was able to get it from a friendly government official or with the help of a high-ranking Christian friend.

Mostly, young women performed the risky job of courier. The Nazis offered rewards to anyone turning in a Jew in hiding, or one trying to pass as a Christian. Even with an identity card, a courier faced the possibility of being recognized by someone and being turned in. Or faced the possibility that her identity card would be discovered as a fake. Men couriers were fewer in number because their risk was greater. Jewish men are circumcised. The Nazis, in their searches for Jews, examined men closely.

Outside the ghettos, the war raged on. At the same time, more German factories were opening to supply Germany's war requirements. Tanks, planes, guns and ammunition were in constant need. So were more common products such as clothing. Ghettos, with their thousands of prisoners, provided a labor reservoir. German factories opened in the ghettos in order to be near a source of labor. Factories in the Warsaw ghetto made brushes, brooms, and wooden shoes. Some Jews found work in these factories. They were the lucky ones. Most met a different fate.

Bombs fell continuously. Destroyed roads and railroad tracks prevented German soldiers and supplies from reaching their destinations. Jewish men in the ghetto between the ages of fourteen—sometimes twelve—and sixty were required to register to work. Each morning, slave labor battalions were marched out of the ghetto under guard. They were put to work repairing roads and railroad tracks, digging canals and ditches, building or rebuilding damaged buildings, hauling bricks and bags of cement. They had to work without a stop. Brutal overseers beat them with whips to keep up the pace. This routine was also in keeping with the Nazi policy of killing as many Jews as possible by natural means. The Jewish slave laborers were worked to death.

The nightmare in the ghetto went along in this way. But it did not end there.

CHAPTER FIVE

Stage Two Begins

The first death camp, at a village called Chelmno, was scheduled to begin operations in December of 1941. But Hitler was impatient with the slow progress of the unmentionable "final solution." He wanted it speeded up. And in May, the SS began to make special arrangements.

Hitler was also impatient for expansion. On June 22, 1941, the German army invaded and occupied a part of Russia. The length and breadth of the territory was to become a vast cemetery. Behind the victorious German army were Heydrich's *Einsatzgruppen*—the special duty groups. That name was another Nazi cover-up code word. The *Einsatzgruppen* were killing squads, mobile murder units. As the army moved out of an area to fight elsewhere, the *Einsatzgruppen* came in and took over.

Heydrich's *Einsatzgruppen* had been coached and prepared and were ready. Stage two of the overall plan for annihilation began with them. With the assistance of local collaborators, largely Lithuanians and Ukrainians, they organized *Aktions*—another code word that meant machine-gunning masses of people to death. They massacred the Jews of every town and village in occupied Russia. And hundreds and thousands of Jews of Kiev, Riga, Vilna, Kovno, Dvinsk, Lvov, and city after city. In July alone, they rounded up and murdered ten thousand Kishinev Jews.

An *Aktion* worked in this way. The Nazis came to a town, rounded up the Jewish families, and told them they were being sent away for "resettlement." The Jews were then led at gunpoint to a large pit at the edge of town, out of sight of witnesses. The pit was a mass grave. If it had not already been dug, the Nazis made the Jews dig their own graves. The Jewish families were ordered to undress and stand at the edge of the pit, then the Nazis shot them in the back of the head. Bodies that had not fallen into the pit were kicked inside. Why the undressing? Naked people are afraid, ashamed, and unable to run. Also, the clothes were washed and sent back to Germany for distribution there.

The Nazis had another system for large crowds. They ordered one group to lie down on the bottom of the pit, shot them, threw earth over them, ordered a second group to lie down on top of the first, and shot *them*. When they had a few layers of corpses, they covered the graves with dirt. Occasionally, a shot failed to kill someone. At night, after the Nazis had left, a person would struggle up over the corpses and escape—to the woods, or to the nearest ghetto.

The *Einsatzgruppen* seemed not to mind murdering Jewish males. But some complained about having to shoot women and children. Their superiors provided them with gas vans—regular vans equipped with shower heads through which gas could be pumped. After undressing, the Jews were ordered into the van, some ninety people at a time, for a shower.

When the doors were closed, the exhaust fumes of the diesel engine were turned on, killing those inside.

The complaining *Einsatzgruppen* did not like this system either. They found the job of removing the corpses messy. The *Einsatzgruppen* were ordered to return to shooting, but the gas method of killing was not abandoned. It would be improved upon and come in for wide use.

The *Einsatzgruppen* did not rely only on shooting. Some experimented with other means. SS officer Magill was in charge of an *Aktion* in the Ukraine. He wrote to his superiors about an experiment of his own that had failed:

> The driving of women and children into the marshes did not have the expected success, because the marshes were not so deep that one could sink.

Magill reported his successes, writing that his units had shot some 6,526 people in the period between July 27 and August 11, 1941. He also described the helpfulness of the local people:

> The Ukrainian clergy were very cooperative and made themselves available for every Aktion. The general population seemed to be on good terms with the Jewish sector. Nevertheless, they helped energetically in rounding up the Jews.

Some Jews were tipped off about roundups and were able to act in time to save their lives. The Jaget family of Lvov were among these. Mrs. Jaget offered to give a farmer her house after the war if he would hide her family. The farmer agreed. He put up a false wall in his cellar. In the false room thus created, the Jaget family, seven-year-old twin boys, Jack and Phil, and eleven-year-old Cecelia, went into hiding. The Gestapo came looking for the Jaget family but did not find them. The family was lucky, but not out of danger. The Nazis always came back. The farmer moved the family, this time to a false room he had made under the pigsty—little more than a cave. And there the Jaget family lived for twenty-two months, receiving from the farmer each Thursday under cover of darkness a food allotment for the week —black bread, cheese, and fat.

Most Jews did not escape. On July 31, Goering sent a memo to Heydrich following up on earlier orders and instructing him to organize "a final solution of the Jewish question in the German sphere of influence."

Heydrich's *Einsatzgruppen* had been annihilating Jews in community after community in Russia. They were to start preparing to do the same elsewhere. But their work in Russia and Poland was not yet finished. The savage shootings continued.

Heydrich told Himmler on August 1 that "there will be no more Jews in the annexed Eastern Territories." It was not an idle boast. The following month, in one location alone, the *Einsatzgruppen,* after only two days of shooting, murdered 33,771 Jews, this time at Babi Yar. By the end of the war, the *Einsatzgruppen,* with the help of local collaborators, had murdered close to two million Jews.

News of the massacres began to reach the ghettos. Because the events were unbelievable, even unimaginable, some people felt it necessary to keep a record, for the sake of history. In the Warsaw ghetto, Emmanuel Ringelblum, a historian, lived with his wife and son. Ringelblum recorded the events that reached him via couriers or via Jews who had escaped from a massacre:

- In all Lithuanian towns, Jews were burned in the streets.
- Jews of Plock awakened in the middle of the night and were driven outdoors. Those who resisted were shot, others deported to Konskie. Several dozen arrived in Konskie in pools of blood and with broken arms and legs.
- Rabbi from Wengrow killed on Yom Kippur. Ordered to sweep street and collect refuse in hat. When he bent over, bayoneted by Germans.
- Slaughter reported in Cracow, Tarnow and other cities.

Ringelblum mainly kept a record of the day-to-day life of the ghetto. The ghetto was large—some hundred blocks. A person living on one block could not know what was happening five blocks away. People came to him to report what had transpired on their street. Ringelblum wrote down what they told him, and also what he saw:

- People are so hungry, they snatch bread from equally poor bread sellers. They bite into the bread so it can't be sold.
- The refugees are boiling potato skins. Eating them makes the belly swell.
- Seventy children were found frozen to death in ruined houses.
- A soldier came through in a wagon and stopped to beat a Jewish pedestrian, ordered him to lie down in the mud and kiss the pavement.
- Soldiers got out of a car and beat men, women and children. They smacked a child who fell unconscious. Onlookers cried. The Gestapo pick up a few Jews every day and break their arms or legs.
- The people who eat only soup and dry bread in the public kitchens are dying. There are fewer of them each day.

- German tourists visit the cemetery to stare at the corpses of people who starved to death. Some enjoy the sight, approving of Hitler's annihilation policy.
- Fifty-two people were shot down in the street at night.
- The 164 youngsters from Germany were sent to Treblinka, where most were murdered.
- 8,000 Viennese refugees have arrived.
- Over 800 were awakened in the middle of the night and taken to labor camps, including invalids.
- 17 corpses returned to ghetto from work camp: earless, arms and other limbs twisted. Tortured by Ukrainian guards.
- 45,000 men were supposed to register for work camps. 11,000 failed to show. Small wonder. In the last roundup (assembling men to be taken away to work), every man returned injured and broken.

Ringelblum encouraged others in the ghetto to keep diaries. Chaim A. Kaplan made this note: "The Nazi is not a normal human being, and it is open to question whether he is human at all. Perhaps he is the missing link between man and the animals."

Avraham Levin, in his diary, marveled that Jews clung to life, that they did not commit suicide. He wrote:

"People die in great numbers of starvation, typhoid or dysentery, they are tortured and murdered by the Germans but they do not give up life voluntarily. On the contrary, they are tied to life by all their senses and have one desire: to see the end of the war and outlive Hitler.

It was not to be.

On December 8, 1941, on schedule, the Chelmno death camp, near the city of Lodz, was put into operation. The first victims had arrived the night before, seven hundred Jews from the town of Kolo. They had been told they were being sent to work camps. The following morning, they were placed in vans equipped with gas and gassed to death, some eighty at a time.

At the same time that Chelmno became a death center— in fact, almost at the same moment—the war spread. On December 7, Japan bombed an American naval base at Pearl Harbor, in Hawaii. The United States declared war on Japan on December 8. Japan's war partners, Germany and Italy, declared war on the United States on December 11, and that same day the United States declared war on them in return. The war had spread around the world. The United States and her two fighting partners, England and Russia, were called the *Allies*. Germany and her partners were called the *Axis*.

The stepped-up tempo of the war did not for an instant interfere with the annihilation program. Eichmann was rounding up the Jews of the Lodz ghetto. They were told they were going to be resettled. That they would be given better quarters to live in and be put to work in agriculture or repairing roads. The Jews could not know it was a lie; they were being sent to their deaths in Chelmno, ten thousand of them, seven hundred a day. Five more death camps were being built. Most would be ready within months.

On July 19, 1942, the plan for annihilation leapt forward. Himmler ordered the SS to start emptying all Polish ghettos of Jews. The job was to be completed in six months—by the end of the year. Skilled workers and those who worked in German factories making essential products were to be exempt, along with their families. All others—beginning with children and old people since they were of no practical value —were to be rounded up and "deported."

The SS in Warsaw received orders to "deport" six to ten thousand Jews a day. The Germans often chose Jewish holidays to attack. July 22 was the eve of the Jewish holiday of *Tisha b'Av*—the Ninth of the Jewish month of Av. It was a day of mourning. On that day two thousand years before, Rome had destroyed Jerusalem and the Temple.

Unknown to the Jews, the Treblinka death camp was opening the next day, on July 23. And they would be mourning for themselves as well. On July 22, posters appeared on the ghetto walls announcing that the resettlement would begin at four o'clock that afternoon. The instructions read:

- All Jews are to be resettled in the East.
- Each Jewish settler may take 15 kilograms [33 pounds] of personal belongings
- Valuables such as gold, jewelry, money, etc., may be taken along.
- Enough food for three days should be brought.
- Failure to comply will be punishable by death.

Most Jews read the announcement with dread. They had come to distrust German pronouncements and words like *resettlement*, or *special treatment*. They did not know the details, but they had heard stories about a massacre at Chelmno. And that the Jews of the Lodz ghetto had been sent away for resettlement and had disappeared. There were similar episodes involving old people and children in the Warsaw ghetto itself. They, too, had been taken away for "resettlement"—put on trains destined for the town of Belzec — and never heard from again. Some who had been taken away sent postcards saying they were well. But most people were suspicious of the cards. It was generally believed that they were forgeries, that the Germans had written them, or made others do so.

Some Jews, desperate for hope, told themselves that the resettlement could be true this time because of the war. Besides, they reasoned, life in the ghetto was hell. Any place had to be an improvement.

They looked for reasons to believe the announcement. Why would they tell us to bring food and take our valuables if it wasn't true? they asked.

The poster on the ghetto wall was the last announcement most of them would ever read. They would read isolated words or phrases at the death camp to which they were being sent, but not more.

On schedule, the Germans began to empty the ghetto section by section. The routine was always the same. Armed

Jews in Warsaw wait on the street with their possessions as the "resettlement" program begins. *(Yad Vashem)*

with guns, clubs, and dogs, they and their helpers arrived at an apartment house and called, *"Alles runter! Alle Juden runter!"*—"Everything down! All Jews down!" Frightened parents holding children by the hand, and children clutching a bundle or a library book poured out into the street. A detail of Nazis went upstairs to search the building and make sure it was empty. Some Jews hid in closets and attics, too afraid to leave. The Nazis found them and shot them. When all the buildings had been emptied, the Nazis organized the crowd into columns of five. Then, guns, clubs, and biting dogs at the ready, they marched the Jews to the railroad tracks at the deportation center, the *Umschlagplatz*—transfer point. Whoever moved too slowly or tried to escape was shot.

The *Umschlagplatz* was a vast, empty building with a great open yard. Trains arrived at the building on tracks in the yard. As ordered, the Nazis took away children and old people first.

Alexander Donat, in the ghetto, also kept a diary. He wrote about the daily roundups:

> The shouts of the SS men, the noise of gunfire, the thud of clubs on human flesh, the groans of the wounded and the last *Shema Yisrael* [a Hebrew declaration that in English is, "Hear, O Israel, the Lord is our God, the Lord alone"] of the dying punctuated the monotonous shuffling of weary feet on the pavement. . . . The sight of children, who accounted for a large percentage of each "shipment to the East," was especially unnerving . . . ragged and un-happy, barefoot or in sandals, most without knapsacks of food, or water, and with shaven heads.

Dr. Yanosz Korczak had prepared the two hundred boys and girls in his orphanage for the arrival of the Nazis. Some days before, the children had put on a play for the people of the ghetto—*The Dying Prince,* written by Korczak. Korczak was a doctor, teacher, and well-known writer and radio personality. His special interest was in raising children with self-respect and dignity. Stefania Wilczynska was his long-time assistant.

Dr. Korczak had prepared the children for the "resettlement." When the Nazis burst in, the children took their food parcels and their water canteens, and went outside. They uttered no sound as they lined up in rows of five. The oldest boy took up the orphanage flag, a gold four-leaf clover on a green background, and positioned himself at the front of the group. Dr. Korczak walked behind him, the two youngest children on either side of him, holding the doctor's hand. Stefania Wilczynska was in back. In silence, the entire group —orphans, teachers, nurses—marched together to the *Umschlagplatz.* Korczak knew where the trains were heading. He could have saved himself. Polish friends were prepared to give him false identity papers. But he chose to remain with the children, answering that one doesn't leave a sick child in the middle of the night.

At the *Umschlagplatz,* if the trains had not yet arrived, Nazis and Ukrainian guards, using boards and clubs, pushed/ the Jews into the building to wait. The overflow waited outside in the yard.

The trains that arrived were not passenger trains but cattle cars, which could hold eight horses each. The cars had been adapted for their new use. Each had four windows, two sealed and two covered with barbed wire. Each held two buckets, one with water for drinking, the other for use as a toilet. Into these cars, which could have held about forty people, the Nazis, using the butts of their guns and tree

Deportees peer out through the barbed wire of a cattle car.
(Archives of the YIVO Institute for Jewish Research)

trunks to push, drove thousands of Jews, filling car after car with some hundred people. Those who were slow to enter were shot. Old men prayed as they went in. Some cried, before a club came down on their heads, *"Ani ma'amin"*— "I believe." These are the opening words of a vow that says the messiah is coming to bring peace and harmony to the world. One who repeats the vow affirms the belief. When all cars were full, the doors were bolted from the outside and the train moved away.

Within minutes, another train arrived and the process was repeated, until the quota of Jews for that day had been put on trains.

In the ghetto, people who did not have work permits, those who were not exempt for work reasons, were in a panic. Some tried to escape to the other side of the wall by way of the tunnels and sewers, or by bribery. Or they tried by any means to get Christian identity cards. These means, if successful, also held dangers. Some Poles went hunting for Jews, trying to take advantage of the rewards the Nazis were offering.

The welfare of the children drove people into despair. The Nazis were taking the children away, no one knew where. Some people gave their children to Christian families for safekeeping. Or put them in the care of a church or monastery. Adam and Pela Starkopf had to resort to other means. Live Jews could not leave the ghetto. But dead bodies could be taken outside for burial. The Starkopfs gave their child a sleeping pill and placed her in a coffin. The father met the hearse at the cemetery and there was able to remove the unconscious child from the coffin, and flee with her.

In all the cities and towns of Europe, the same desperate efforts at survival were being made.

Each morning at the ghetto brought the same nightmare. Day after day the call *"Alles runter! Alle Juden runter!"* rang through the buildings and streets. Sometimes, to vary their routine, the Germans shot everyone in sight. Sometimes, instead of bothering to round up old people, they brought them to the Jewish cemetery and shot them. Methodically, systematically, the Nazis emptied the ghetto apartment house by apartment house. If a given section did not turn up the quota of six or ten thousand they had been asked for, they made up the quota by seizing people in the street or pulling them from their homes.

Those in the ghetto whose turn had not yet come watched from the windows. The United States' entry into the war fed their hopes. Others were less optimistic. Chaim A. Kaplan wrote in his diary,

> "Our only good fortune is that our days are numbered—that we shall not live long under such conditions. . . . This death that lurks behind our walls will be our salvation; but there is one thorn. We shall not have the privilege of seeing the downfall of the Nazis."

Still others tried to hide. Some might have made it but for the sound of a crying child that gave them away or the moans of a sick person. Or the thoroughness of Nazi searches.

Jack Eisner remembers such a search. He and his family lived on one street, his grandmother on another. The Nazis were taking away old people—no one knew where. And the family had made a secret room for his grandmother in the attic of her building, where she was in hiding. Fifteen-year-old Jack went to take his grandmother some food one day, when he ran into SS troops and Ukrainian guards with machine guns and dogs conducting a roundup. By dodging them, he arrived at his grandmother's hiding place safely. As they embraced, they heard the dreaded sound of SS boots on the stairs. The grandmother told Jack to hide under the bed, and he did so. A moment later, the Germans stormed into the room, seized the old lady, and flung her down the stairs. Jack never saw his grandmother again.

Who was left in the ghetto? When the roundups started in July, some hundred thousand Jews had died of starvation and disease. Other thousands had been killed in random shootings, or disappeared in labor roundups.

Over three hundred thousand Jews had been rounded up, brought to the *Umschlagplatz,* and packed into trains. The

SS in Warsaw had been given six months to empty the ghetto. To impress their superiors, they had done so in a little over two months.

Remaining in the ghetto were some fifty thousand Jews, men and women who had been kept behind to work in German factories and businesses, and their families. Jack Eisner, his mother, and father were among them. (His teenaged sister had been shot trying to escape during a roundup.) Emmanuel Ringelblum and his family were also among them. So were the members of the Jewish underground. All had been spared—but only temporarily.

CHAPTER SIX

The Warsaw Ghetto Uprising

Underground groups had sprung up in all major ghettos. The first one had appeared in the Vilna ghetto in Lithuania. Near Vilna was the village of Ponary. Such villages, which had few people and therefore few witnesses, were favored by the Nazis as killing sites. Most of the sixty thousand Jews of the Vilna ghetto were slaughtered at Ponary by the *Einsatzgruppen*—the special duty groups, over five thousand in July alone. Standing naked together before open pits, entire families were shot in the head and tossed inside. Some twelve thousand Jews still remained in the Vilna ghetto. Abba Kovner, a poet, was one of the leaders of the underground. His motto "Better to fall with honor in the ghetto than to be led like sheep to Ponary!" became the cry in the Vilna ghetto— and resounded in all ghettos.

A ghetto underground was limited in what it could do. Its members were prisoners. They were surrounded by guards and police and had to operate in secret. The German policy of reprisal also limited their actions. To discourage Jewish rebellion, a policy spelled out earlier by Goebbels was followed: "For every Jewish assassination and for every attempt at revolt on the part of the Jews, 100 or 150 Jews in our hands will be shot." In practice, the numbers often exceeded Goebbels's guidelines. A Jew shot a German policeman near the city of Pinsk. The *Einsatzgruppen* chief reported to his superior that "as a reprisal, 4,500 Jews were liquidated." A Jew in the Lvov ghetto killed a brutal guard. In return, the Germans killed a thousand Jews.

A ghetto underground could not change the course of the war. Mighty nations fighting against Germany had been unable to do so. Still, underground members did what they could to destroy or damage German military installations; to learn what Germans were planning for their own, or another, ghetto; to create underground tunnels as secret exits and secret hiding places. Members of the Cracow ghetto dressed in stolen SS *Waffen* uniforms went into an SS restaurant and left a bomb behind. The restaurant was blown up. Chaika Grossman, a teenaged girl in the Bialystok ghetto, smuggled in weapons and organized underground cells. The underground also acted as a court. Jews who were accused of collaborating with the Germans were tried and executed.

The Jews in the Warsaw ghetto knew that the Germans would be back, that work card or no work card, their days were numbered. They also now knew about the Treblinka death camp. The trains leaving the *Umschlagplatz* returned too quickly. They were supposed to take the Jews to Russia for work. That was far away. They were returning to the *Umschlagplatz* six hours after leaving. It was three hours to Treblinka, and three back.

The Jews of the Warsaw ghetto decided to fight with all they had the next time the Nazis came. They stole and bought guns and ammunition. They prepared false documents for any who might escape.

The dreaded sound of Nazi boots appeared on the pavements on January 18, 1943. The Germans had arrived without warning. By order of Himmler, they had come to round up the remaining Jews. The Jews, taken by surprise, were unprepared. Even so, they fought back and the Germans suffered heavy losses. The losses of the Jews were far greater. When the fighting was over, one thousand Jews had been killed. And sixty-five hundred were taken under guard to the *Umschlagplatz* and put on trains.

Some forty thousand Jews now remained in the ghetto. The underground vowed not to be taken by surprise the next time. And to die fighting, and with honor. They gave out leaflets telling the people of the ghetto: *Defend yourselves. Grab an axe, an iron bar, a knife.* The people agreed. They let young men and women fighters of the underground, some seven hundred of them, make plans.

The underground stole and bought more rifles. They made hand grenades and small bombs by filling bottles with stolen explosives. They collected boards, sticks, anything that could strike a blow. They smuggled in supplies of food, and constructed bunkers and hiding places for the people to live in and for themselves to shoot from. Underground headquarters were at Mila 18. Twenty-four-year-old Mordekai Anielewicz, the commander, operated from there. Under him, other young men and women were in charge elsewhere in the ghetto.

In February, Himmler ordered complete destruction of the ghetto. The Nazis announced to the Jews that there would be another "resettlement." They knew the Jews were suspicious of the word, so they did it a little differently this time. The SS told the German bosses, for whom the Jews worked, what to say. And the bosses passed the word along, telling the Jewish workers that this time the "resettlement" was for real. And that they would be smart to go along. The Jews paid no attention to the lie. They went into hiding. Taking supplies of food and water, men, women, and children holed up in the cellars, sewers, and underground bunkers and tunnels.

With orders from Himmler to crush the Jews, the Nazis attacked on April 19, 1943, at the start of the holiday of Passover. Two thousand armed SS troops entered the ghetto, marching with tanks, rifles, machine guns, and trailers full of ammunition. The Jewish fighters were in position—in bunkers, in windows, on rooftops. They had rifles and handguns, hand grenades and bombs that they had made. And they let fly.

Passover is celebrated by reciting the Bible story of Exodus. The Jews in the Warsaw ghetto had baked the traditional matzah bread eaten on that holiday, hoping to be able to celebrate. They munched on matzah and celebrated as they fought. Pulling triggers, throwing grenades, dodging bullets, they shouted to each other over the gunfire the events of the Exodus, telling how Moses freed the Jewish slaves in Egypt and led them out to freedom.

Unbelievably, the Jews won the battle that day. The Germans were forced to retreat. The battle resumed the next day, and the Germans were again forced to retreat. The Germans brought in more troops, and the fighting intensified. German pilots dropped bombs on the ghetto. On April 23, under the command of General Juergen Stroop, the Germans set fire to the ghetto. Jews leapt from windows to escape the flames. Others died of smoke inhalation. The Jews were running out of food and water, and of strength and ammunition. Those who could do so fought on.

On May 1, Goebbels wrote in his diary:

> [There is] exceptionally sharp fighting in Warsaw between our police, and in part even the Air Force, and the Jewish rebels. The Jews have actually succeeded in putting the ghetto in a condition to defend itself. Some very hard battles are taking place there. . . . Of course this jest will probably not last long.

He added a complaint. "But it shows what one can expect of the Jews if they have guns."

Goebbels' tone was mocking. But his forecast was inevitable—and correct. On May 8, the Germans surrounded the Jewish underground headquarters at Mila 18. Anielewicz and 150 fighters were trapped inside. They discussed the situation. Rather than fall into German hands, they killed one another.

On May 16, Stroop proudly sent a report to Himmler saying, *The Jewish quarter of Warsaw is no more!* He amplified: Seven thousand Jews had been killed in fighting, thirty thousand had been put on trains, and several hundred had perished in the flames.

Goebbels did not record in his diary, when the uprising was over, that the starving Jews of the ghetto, with their pathetic supply of arms, had held out against the German army for some forty days, longer than Poland or France had held out.

The rebellion was all but over. Some Jews remained hidden in underground passages and continued to fight. Others

Warsaw Jews, captured during the rebellion, are led off by the Nazis. *(The Bettmann Archive)*

had managed to crawl through the tunnels and sewers to the other side of the wall, to safety in the Christian side of Warsaw. They had prepared for it and carried false identity cards identifying them as Catholics. Emmanuel Ringelblum and his family were among these. They would be discovered by the Germans and killed.

In Ringelblum's view, the Jews were disappearing from the face of the earth. The outside world knew nothing of it and had no way of learning about what happened. His diaries explained everything. He had been hiding his secret diaries all along, burying them in metal boxes and rubber-sealed milk cans in and around the ghetto. The hope was that Germany would lose the war and the Allies would find the diaries and learn the secret history.

Other fighters escaped into the woods and forests. These places were full of underground fighters, partisans of different political groups and different countries. Some were Jewish groups. Most were Christian, fighting against German occupation of their countries. Many Jews who escaped into the woods joined one or another of these underground groups. Young Jack Eisner joined a Christian group in the woods. He had to pretend to be a Christian since Christian groups were often hostile to Jews.

The news about the revolt of the Jews in the Warsaw ghetto had spread to other ghettos. The Jews of the Vilna ghetto in Lithuania were proud of the Jews of Warsaw. Hirsh Glick, another poet, was inspired to write a song of hope. It was widely sung then and is a classic song today:

> You must never say you walk the final mile
> Because darkness for now covers heaven's smile.
> The hour that we long for's drawing near,
> Our step beats out the message: We are here.

A few months later, in September, the Germans rounded up the Jews of the Vilna ghetto, marched them to the *Umschlagplatz,* and put them also on trains. The ghettos were empty. Every Jewish man, woman, and child had been, or was being, put on a train.

The doors of the train were bolted on the outside. The Jews near the windows looked out through barbed wire, not knowing where they were or where they were heading. The packed, stifling, filthy trains sometimes stopped for days. The

Jews ran out of food and water. The Nazis sometimes allowed them to get off the train during the wait. They were able to relieve themselves at such times, or, when the Nazis were not watching, beg food and water of the local people.

Where were the trains heading? For the six death camps of Chelmno, Treblinka, Sobibor, Auschwitz, Belzec, Maidanek—named after the towns in which they were located—dreaded names to this day.

Dr. Korczak, the orphans, the diary writers, the smugglers, teachers, musicians, entertainers, the Jewish police, the grandparents, parents, and children, all the more than three hundred thousand Jews of the Warsaw ghetto were brought to the Treblinka death camp and murdered on the same day that they arrived. The Jews of the Bialystok ghetto were also murdered there and in Maidanek as well. The Jews of Lublin were murdered at Sobibor, Belzec, and Maidanek. The Jews of Cracow, in Sobibor and at other camps. And so it went for the Polish Jews.

But not only Polish Jews were on the trains. The Germans had emptied all Jewish ghettos, all over Europe. And all day long trains rolled into Poland, bringing thousands of Jews to one death camp or another. They brought Russian-Jewish women and children from Lvov and Jews from France. They brought Jews from Czechoslovakia, Belgium, Yugoslavia, Latvia, Luxembourg, and Italy. Also Jews from seven ghettos in Greece, in trains so packed the people had to stand for days. The trains brought to Sobibor one hundred thousand Dutch Jews from the Westerbork concentration camp in Holland. There were one thousand "pieces" to a car, as the Nazis had put it in their report. All were murdered on arrival.

Polish Jews who had been suffering under the Nazis for years suspected where the trains were heading. They had few illusions about the fate that awaited them. Most Jews from other countries believed the lies they had been told. They thought they were going to a camp to work. Or to a transit camp. Why not? Germany was in dire need of laborers to keep its factories, plants, and farms going. If they worked well, the Jews told themselves, and made themselves useful, all would go well for them. They had prepared for the journey and marked their suitcases with their names, as the SS had instructed them to do. The sign over the entrance at Auschwitz further convinced them. It read: *Arbeit Macht Frei*—Work Makes a Person Free. They never dreamed, when the train pulled in, that they were arriving in a killing center. How could they? The thought was unimaginable. It had never been thought before.

CHAPTER SEVEN

Auschwitz-Birkenau

All death camps were much the same. The routine in one was the general routine in another. With one exception. Five camps existed only for killing — an entire trainload of people was murdered on arrival. Auschwitz-Birkenau was different. It was a death camp and also a labor camp. Most people were murdered on arrival. But a quantity, some 20 percent of every trainload, were kept alive for purposes of slave labor.

Auschwitz and Birkenau (Birch Wood) were some two miles apart and linked by rail. They were the principal camps in a complex containing Manowicz and other labor camps. German factories that made synthetic oil, synthetic rubber, explosives, windows, doors, and other items were set up in these camps. German coal mines were also nearby. Slave laborers were assigned to work in these factories and mines.

Auschwitz-Birkenau was spread out, with many buildings. A man could not know that his wife was a prisoner in the women's barracks. A woman could not know that her sister

The sign over the entrance gate to Auschwitz read: Work Makes a Person Free. *(Yad Vashem)*

was working nearby. It was the largest of the killing centers. Auschwitz itself had one killing unit — an undressing hall, a gas chamber, and a crematorium with three ovens. Birkenau was the main killing site, with four units — two with large gas chambers and crematoria with many ovens in each.

The Nazis had "improved" on the killing systems used by the *Einsatzgruppen* earlier. The mass graves had caused problems. For one thing, body gasses escaped after a while and made cracks in the earth. People living in the area complained about the stench. This led to giving away the secret of the "final solution." The secret was further threatened as the war brought the Russian army closer. If Russian troops discovered the mass graves, the secret would be out.

To prevent that from happening, the mass graves at Pon-

These women and children have just arrived at Auschwitz by train.
(Yad Vashem)

ary, near Vilna, those near Lvov, at Babi Yar, near Kiev, in
the Borki Woods, near Chelm, and elsewhere were dug up
and the bodies burned. Jewish prisoners were used for the
job. Former *Einsatzgruppen* SS Colonel Paul Blobel super-
vised "Operation Blot-Out." SS men armed with machine
guns and killer dogs stood over the Jewish laborers, as,
shackled around the ankles, they opened graves, dug up
corpses, piling them up sometimes thirty-five hundred to a
pyre, and set fire to the pyre.

Szloma Gol and his group dug up sixty-eight thousand
corpses. The Nazis had assigned two men in the labor bat-
talion to do nothing but count bodies. In September 1941,
ten thousand Jews of the Vilna ghetto had been rounded up
and taken to be shot. Gol's brother had been among them.

They were all here. Gol found his brother's corpse among them. Others also found relatives in the same way. The Nazis would not give up the system of mass burial. They would "improve" upon it.

The Nazis had also "improved" upon the gassing system.

Rudolf Hoess, a convicted murderer and former prison official, was the first commandant of Auschwitz. Himmler had sent for Hoess in the summer of 1941 to discuss the Jewish problem. After the war, Hoess told an international court:

> The "final solution" of the Jewish question meant the complete extermination of all Jews in Europe. I was ordered to establish extermination facilities at Auschwitz in June 1941.
>
> . . . I visited Treblinka to find out how they carried out their extermination. The Camp Commandant told me that he had liquidated 80,000 in the course of one-half year. He was principally concerned with liquidating all the Jews from the Warsaw ghetto. He used monoxide gas.

Hoess found the system at Treblinka flawed. Only about two hundred people at a time could be killed there. Some victims were still alive after the gassing. Furthermore, the victims knew they were going to be gassed. The kicking and screaming slowed down the killing process and made it more difficult.

Hoess made "improvements" at Auschwitz. He put fruit trees around the killing units and introduced various niceties to deceive the Jews. And he switched to Zyklon B, a fast-acting poison that killed by suffocation. He was able to kill some two thousand people at a time in each of the large chambers. And, when all the ovens were working, he could incinerate 4,756 bodies in twenty-four hours.

Hoess bragged at the trial that in the time that he was in charge, Auschwitz gassed two-and-a-half million people and killed another half million by starvation and disease. He also bragged about SS thoroughness. Children arriving at Auschwitz who were too young or too weak to work were murdered at once. Desperate mothers tried to hide their small children under their clothes. Hoess reported, "Of course when we found them we sent the children to be exterminated." When asked by a lawyer how he could have done such things, he answered:

> Being a member of the SS and obedient to the discipline of that organization, I believed that all orders issued by its leader [Himmler] and by Hitler were right . . . and it would have been a disgrace and a weakness on my part had I refused in any way to carry out their orders.

Railroad tracks in Germany, Holland, France, Belgium, Italy, and various points in Poland led directly to Auschwitz. And each day, the trains came, bringing in thirty to fifty cars at a time, carrying thousands of Jews. Many had died on the way of starvation, asphyxiation, or illness. Those who arrived were hungry, thirsty, exhausted, and anxious. Some wondered if they would really be better off in this work camp. Others were bewildered. If they were going to work on a farm in Estonia or another country, as they believed, why were they in Poland?

The people standing near the windows could see that barbed wire surrounded the camp. If they suspected that the wire was electrified, they would have been right. Out of

The sign says: Beware! High voltage. Dangerous! *(AP/Wide World Photos)*

range of their vision was a prisoner, a man in a striped uniform, rigid and staring, his hand still on the wire that had electrocuted him as he — tried to escape? Or was flung against the wire by guards, to be killed?

They could see towers around the camp, and guards with machine guns in the towers. They could see several armed SS and a dozen or so non-German guards standing around the station. Not very many people to guard thousands of prisoners. No more were needed. The guards had guns, clubs, and killer dogs on leashes. Terror is worth a thousand guards.

As a train came to a halt, the guards boarded, yelling, "Out! Out! Jews get out!" The guards threw out the corpses and ordered everyone off the train, yelling and shouting: "Hurry!" "Make it fast!" "Faster!" They poked with rifle butts and clubs to hasten people along. The dazed and stricken prisoners hurried as best they could, trying to avoid the clubs. A command came over the loudspeaker, announcing: "Men to the right! Women to the left!" Husbands, brothers, and sons went one way. Mothers with small children, sisters, and daughters went the other. Most would never see each other again.

Also meeting the trains were high Nazi officials. In May 1943, Dr. Joseph Mengele, a captain in the SS, was the chief medical officer of Auschwitz. To serve Hitler's ideal of a master race, Mengele performed medical experiments on people. Twins, because they were doubles, were of special interest to him. If he could have found the secret of twins, he would have been able to double the German population. Mengele experimented on twins, some fifteen hundred of which were Jewish. Two hundred lived through the war. Mengele also injected dye into the eyes of brown-eyed people, trying to make the eyes blue. He and other German doctors also experimented on the inmates in other ways. When their bodies were no longer useful, the people were killed.

Mengele had come to the trains in order to make "selections." The scene over which he presided was filled with frightened, weeping people as wives looked about for their husbands, as mothers looked for sons and tried to hide their babies. Survivors reported after the war that separation from loved ones was the greatest agony in the nightmare.

As the guards poked with their clubs, pushing people into this group or that, ghostly looking men in striped uniforms with shaven heads appeared with carts. The men, emaciated and barely able to stand, were prisoner-porters. They had come for the luggage. The Jews were told over a loudspeaker that after they had registered, they would receive back their luggage. There was no truth to the announcement. It was a false nicety, a ruse designed to keep them calm and make them manageable. The Jews would never see their luggage again. The clothing would be sorted — suits, coats, dresses, shoes and underwear — men's, women's, and children's. It would all be cleaned in the laundry and shipped to Germany.

Sometimes a prisoner-porter dared to approach a group when a guard was not looking. He might whisper, "Run away!" or "Fight! We are too weak," trying to warn the people. But in the chaos and confusion the new arrivals did not understand the warning. At the same time, guards were pushing with their clubs, ordering them to hurry, as the voice over the loudspeaker told them to form into rows of five for "selection." The voice explained what that meant. The strongest would be selected for work; the old and sick would be sent to the infirmary; all others would receive showers and be taken care of.

Numbered rows allowed the Nazis to keep order and keep track of prisoners. And as the Jews hurried to obey and form themselves into rows of five, they could see emaciated people in striped uniforms, women with shaven heads who did not look like women, men who were little more than skeletons. An orchestra of prisoner musicians played classical music. That nicety, too, was designed to deceive people into thinking that they had arrived at a pleasant place.

The new arrivals could also see a chimney spitting dark smoke into the sky. And the putrid smell! They could not know that it was the smell of burning flesh. Their thoughts were elsewhere. They were dirty and starving, exhausted and frightened. They looked forward to the promises contained in signs that read Barbers, Cloak Room, Valuables, To Baths and Inhalators.

The SS and the guards, eternally prodding with guns and clubs, marched the first columns of five before Dr. Mengele for "selection." The process moved quickly. The routine had been established. Old people, mothers with small children, pregnant women, and all children under ten or eleven, depending on their size, were to be gassed at once. Mengele glanced at an individual. If he or she was one of the above, he jerked his thumb to the right. If a person looked strong enough to work, he jerked his thumb to the left.

The street orphans coming before Mengele tried to get chosen for work. Some stretched their necks, to make themselves look taller. Some pleaded to be permitted to work. But Mengele only pointed to the right and glanced at the next person.

Sometimes a porter's whispered warning was heard and understood in time. A porter sidled up to fourteen-year-old Hugo Gryn, standing with his mother, father, and eleven-year-old brother. The porter murmured to Hugo, "You're eighteen, you have a trade," then repeated the same thing to another boy. Hugo thought the man was crazy. But Hugo's father did not. He told Hugo to say just that. And when the SS man asked Hugo how old he was, he answered accordingly. And he said he was a carpenter, when asked if he had a trade. Hugo and his parents were sent to the left, the brother to the right. Mrs. Gryn tried to go with the younger boy, to remain with him. But the SS shoved her to the left, saying she would be joining the boy soon enough. Hugo never saw his brother again.

Although the pain of separation was great for new arrivals, some people were glad when their sick relatives were taken away in a truck to the infirmary in the distance, over which a Red Cross flag flew. They could not know that that was no infirmary. The flag flew over a large, open pit. The people taken there were made to sit on the edge of the pit, then were shot in the back of the neck.

CHAPTER EIGHT

Those on the Right

Quickly, women with children marching in columns of five were led to the "showers" — to be disinfected and made clean after their journey. As guards hurried them along, and as the ghostly orchestra played, they were brought to a large hall and told to undress.

The columns of men would be sent to a different undressing hall. They would have the same experience. As the men were undressing in their hall, and the women and children in theirs, the contents of their luggage were being cleaned and sorted for shipment to Germany.

Signs in the undressing hall read: Clean Is Good, Lice Can Kill, Wash Yourself. Crude, insulting even. But, under the circumstances, perhaps not out of place. Next, the women were told to turn their valuables over to the guards for safe-keeping. The women would never again see their wedding rings, lockets, watches, or eyeglasses.

Gold taken from the prisoners was melted down and sent to Germany, along with precious stones and other valuables.

An elderly woman and young children being sent to the "showers."
(Yad Vashem)

Some watches and other valuable items were kept in camp stores, to be used as Christmas presents for and by the SS. A shipment of goods taken from Jews in the death camps was sent to Himmler on April 30, 1943. The Nazis kept careful records: There were 94,000 men's watches, 33,000 women's watches, 25,000 fountain pens, 14,000 automatic pencils, and 14,000 scissors.

The men were led naked from the undressing halls, directly to the "showers." Women first lost their hair. Camp barbers came, cut off the hair of some fifty or sixty women, then started on the next batch. The Nazis laughed at the sight of the women they had degraded, naked and without hair. Amusement was a side benefit. They did it for practical reasons. They sold human hair to German companies that used it in mattress stuffing, coat linings, and slippers.

The women and children were hurried toward a building where the words *Wash and Disinfection Room* appeared on the door. They could not know that this was a gas chamber. Or that the ambulance parked nearby stored poison gas. Or that the barbed wire fence woven with leafy branches hid a crematorium, where corpses were burned. Up to the last minute, the SS deceived the women with normal-sounding phrases: "Tie both shoes well, and put your clothing in one pile, because they will be handed back to you at the end of the showers." And telling them, if they asked for water, that coffee was being prepared, and if they did not hurry the coffee would be cold.

"Hurry! Hurry!" the guards yelled, prodding with whips,

Ovens at Auschwitz. *(Yad Vashem)*

bayonets, and clubs, pushing women and children into the "shower." Some women outside became suspicious and refused to go in. The guards beat them and sicked dogs on them, forcing them in until the chamber was packed. If there were any children left outside, the guards took them by an arm or leg and flung them inside, over the heads of the others, then screwed the doors shut. Inside, pellets of poisoned gas were dropped into the chamber from a shower head on the ceiling. Fifteen or twenty minutes later, everyone inside was dead.

Corpses were removed from a door on the other side of the gas chamber. This was done by some two hundred Jewish prisoners called *Sonderkommando*—special squads. Under the watchful eyes of the guards, the *Sonderkommando* examined the corpses for hidden jewelry. Gold teeth were pulled out, melted down, and sent to the Nazi bank in Germany. The *Sonderkommando* then loaded the corpses onto small, open cars standing on rails nearby and carted them to the ovens.

Not a moment was wasted. While the cars were carrying away the corpses, the gas chamber was being washed and cleaned and made ready for the next columns of five. The process moved quickly.

The ashes were buried or used as a spread on roads to prevent slipping. Or they were used as fertilizer for the flower beds around the offices of the SS. Or thown into a body of water. Tracks led from crematoria 4 and 5 to a nearby pond. Ashes were dumped there. Auschwitz is today a museum. A booklet issued to visitors by the Polish government says ashes are visible to this day.

The trains that brought the new arrivals did not leave Auschwitz empty. They left carrying slave laborers to work in Germany or elsewhere.

CHAPTER NINE

Those on the Left

Most of the men and women selected for labor worked in one of the German factories or mines, or on construction projects for the SS or German army. Or at the death factory of Auschwitz itself. They were allowed to remain alive only so long as they were able to work. When they could no longer do so, they were gassed to death. Himmler had laid down the fate of slave laborers in work camps: "Even from there the Jews are some day to disappear, in accordance with the Fuehrer's wishes."

Even in Auschwitz, where killing was a full-time job, the Nazis tried to keep the killings secret. They could not, however, keep the secret from the *Sonderkommando*. But they could keep the *Sonderkommando* from talking. And this the Nazis did by isolating them from other prisoners. The men of *Sonderkommando* were permitted to work for a few months, then were gassed to death. The Nazis had no need to fear a labor shortage. Trains arrived daily carrying thousands of new prisoners.

Sonderkommando was one of the jobs at Auschwitz.

(Above) Having escaped death at least for the moment, these women have been chosen for labor and have had their heads shaved. *(Yad Vashem)*

(Below) After receiving camp uniforms, women march to work. *(Yad Vashem)*

Other workers, besides porters and barbers, were sorters of confiscated items, packers, carpenters, plumbers, latrine cleaners, laundry and kitchen workers, gardeners and house servants for the SS, and performers of other such services.

Before being assigned to work, prisoners received numbers. The numbers were tattooed on their forearms with blue ink. The men's hair was shorn, and they were sent to take showers. Everyone received prison clothes: a ragged, ill-fitting striped uniform for the men and a striped dress and jacket for the women, one set of underwear, and one pair of wooden clogs, or shoes. They slept in the clothes that they had worked in all day.

Men and women occupied separate barracks. A barracks accommodated some eight hundred people. Prisoners slept in three-tiered bunks, about eight to a bunk. The bunks were lined with old straw, a mat, or nothing. The barracks was foul-smelling, dirty, cold and damp year-round. In winter, prisoners were chilled through and through. The floor was covered with mud and slime trekked in from the outside. There was a bucket of water for drinking. The water was to be used sparingly. It was. Insects, dirt, and all. Water for daily washing was also a problem. People tried to catch rainwater in their drinking cups.

Prisoners needing to relieve themselves had to ask the barracks guard for permission. Or they went with their group at the appointed time to the latrine. This was a building in which a long board with holes had been set over a trench. Prisoners went in a few at a time, and were told to hurry so the next group could go in. Sometimes a huge barrel outside a barracks served as a latrine, sometimes a couple of buckets between the barracks.

Men were put in special barracks for six to eight weeks

for daily drills before being sent to work. The drills were designed to break their spirit and turn them into obedient servants. They were beaten and made to walk on broken glass and sing at the same time. They were made to run, jump, and crawl for hours at a time, and turn around on their knees while they knelt on gravel or sharp pebbles.

Many died during this period. Some killed themselves by throwing themselves against the electrified barbed wire. But most Jews would not commit suicide. They refused to do so as an act of rebellion, since committing suicide would be helping Hitler in his plan. Others clung to hope. They hoped to live just one more day, then one more. In a day, the war could come to an end.

The men who survived the drill period were assigned to work. Often, they did not survive the assignment. Especially those working outdoors. In winter, in the snow, they worked without coats and often without shoes. Many were carted away half dead in wheelbarrows at the end of the day. One doctor worked in the first aid room of a factory, about two miles from his camp. He and other men had to march to and from work each day in rows of five. He later told of his experiences:

> Besides [the long walk] we had to stand during roll-call which lasted from one to two hours. Under such conditions it was possible to survive three to four months; people died of exhaustion and overwork. About 500 to 600 patients came to the surgery each day. There were cases of severe beating at work and every day about ten persons were brought dead or half-dead, the latter died soon after.

Many of those chosen for labor died of starvation. They received some thirteen hundred to seventeen hundred calories daily, less than what is needed for a body at rest. Breakfast was black coffee or herb tea with a little sugar. Lunch was potato, turnip, or cabbage soup. For supper, there was coffee and a piece of bread with a small slice of sausage, margarine, jam, or cheese. Even these meager allotments were not always available. Prisoners were always hungry. Grown men and women were emaciated and had the bodies of children. A German servant of a high-ranking SS officer testified after the war that the SS stole prisoners' rations and sent food parcels to their relatives in Germany.

Often the soup given to prisoners was inedible. Kitty Hart was a young Polish Jewish woman in Auschwitz. She and other women in her group were marched out of the camp under guard at 6:00 A.M. They were given spades and set to work digging a trench. It was summer, and they had no shelter from the sun. Women supervisors with sticks hovered over them to make sure they kept working. At noon, the lunch whistle blew. Kitty and the other women were forbidden to move. They sat in groups of five, watching as huge soup cauldrons were brought in for them.

> When the lid of our cauldron came off the nauseating smell reached us from yards away. But we were desperate for some kind of food. This time the soup was made of nettles, with some green and yellow bits floating on top.

The men and women who worked in factories fared somewhat better since the work was performed indoors. But they faced other hardships. Prisoners worked twelve hours a day, with half an hour for lunch. They received the usual thin soup and a piece of bread. They were given a quota of work to turn out each day. If they fell short, they were beaten. If they worked too slowly, they were beaten. Since the Germans considered Jews inferior, Jews were not allowed to speak to their bosses. If they had something to say, they had to motion with their hands. If they forgot and spoke, they were punished. Most male and female supervisors were sadists, people who enjoy inflicting pain on others. They did not hesitate to whip, beat, or maim a worker.

At the end of the day, prisoners were marched back to camp for roll call. Roll call was a check to make sure no one had escaped. The Nazis turned roll call into a torture. They made prisoners stand at attention for hours at a time. Sometimes during roll call, to amuse themselves, they made women kneel and at the same time hold their arms in the air.

Prisoners were arrested for the slightest offense or for no offense at all. Stealing food or going to the bathroom without permission were against camp rules. So was owning a towel. Rudolf Fahn found a piece of cloth, which he used to wipe himself after washing. A guard caught him in the washroom and beat him to death on the spot.

Each offense had a punishment. Whipping called for twenty-five strokes. The SS often made the victim keep count in German. If he or she missed, both the whipping and the counting started over from number one.

Those who tried to escape or were suspected of plotting an escape were arrested and questioned. To make the prisoners talk, the Nazis pulled out fingernails, inserted needles into the sensitive parts of a woman's body, or poured water down a prisoner's throat through a funnel. Prisoners who were to be executed were lined up facing a wall in the courtyard and left to stand there all day, until the evening roll call. They were shot at that time so everyone could hear — and see — what happened to them. Hanging was another means of execution. The gallows were near the kitchen, also so everyone could see the swinging bodies. The Germans made it a point to hang Jews "in the presence of their race."

How did the Jews in the camps endure the horrors they had to face daily? How did they survive?

Itka Frajman Zygmuntowicz was a teenager at Auschwitz. She saw the SS torture her mother for withholding information. Itka vowed never to join the forces of evil, never to become like "them." And to live — or die — with dignity. Luck, and dreams of freedom, helped keep her alive. She fed her dream by writing poetry. Not with a pencil, for she had none. But in her head. After the war, she wrote down the poems. The first stanza of "A Bird With Clipped Wings" reads:

> I feel like a bird with clipped wings
> tied to this earth by invisible strings
> chained to a destiny I did not choose,
> I feel like a prisoner who cannot break loose.

Dr. William Glicksman's wife, child, and sister had been murdered by the Nazis during a roundup. He had worked at draining swamps and was interrogated and beaten by the Nazis, and put to work in the munitions plant. After the war, his answer to the question of how one survived was:

> I stayed alive through spiritual strength. We never forgot for a minute that we were Jews.... On a Friday night, we sang quietly "Lecha Nerannena" [Come, let us sing before the Lord] while sitting at our workbenches. Right under the eyes of the German supervisor we said kaddish [the prayer for the dead] for Herzl [a Zionist leader]. We talked about Bialik and Achad Ha'Am [Jewish writers] — that is how we lasted until evacuation on January 18.

Hitler and the Nazis never let up in their war against the Jews. The killing continued until the last days, even moments, of the war. The trains kept coming, bringing Jewish men, women, and children from Holland, Vienna, Trieste, Berlin, Greece, and elsewhere. They brought three hundred children from the Polish town of Kovno and four thousand children from France. They brought 1,196 children and 53 doctors from the Theresienstadt ghetto in Czechoslovakia. All were brought to the gas chamber the same day that they arrived. Throughout, the Nazis continued to gloss over the "final solution" among themselves, and to speak in code. Himmler, speaking to a gathering of his officers in October, 1943, made an exception one day:

> Among ourselves, this once, we will speak of it openly here, but we must never talk about it in public. Most of you know what it means to see 100 corpses piled up, or 500 or 1,000. To have gone through this and — except for instances of human weakness — to have remained decent, that has made us tough. This is a glorious page in our unwritten and never-to-be-written history.

He expressed other Nazi beliefs:

> One basic principle must be absolute for the SS man. We must be honest, decent, loyal and comradely to members of our own blood and to nobody else. What happens to the Russians, the Czechs, is a matter of total indifference to me. What there is in the nations in the way of good blood of our kind, we will take for ourselves — if necessary, by kidnapping their children and raising them among us. Whether other nations live in prosperity or croak from hunger interests me only in so far as we need them as slaves for our culture.

He ended his speech by saying:

> We want to be worthy of having been permitted to be the first SS men of the Fuehrer, Adolf Hitler, in the long history of the Germanic people which stretches before us. We now direct our thoughts to the Fuehrer, our Fuehrer, Adolf Hitler, who will create the Germanic Reich and will lead us into the Germanic future.

Himmler did not know that the Germanic future he foresaw was drawing to a close. Already, Germany had suffered reverses earlier in the year. In February, the German army fighting in Russia had been forced to surrender. In July, Allied troops invaded Italy.

On the other front, the one against the Jews, there had also been disturbances. The Jews in the death camps were rebelling. Also those in the labor camps. With stolen grenades, pickaxes, hammers, and stones, they were attacking their guards and Nazi overseers. Offenders were machine-gunned to death. Rebellions were put down. The heroic but pathetic rebellions could not change the course of that war — Hitler's war against the Jews.

By the end of the year, except for Auschwitz, the death camps had ceased their killing operations. Their task had been completed. The regions around them were *Judenrein*.

Survivors of a Nazi concentration camp in Austria liberated on May 7, 1945. *(The Bettmann Archive)*

CHAPTER TEN

The War Ends

At long last, early in 1944, the war turned in favor of the Allies. Soviet troops were sweeping across Poland. British and American planes were bombing and destroying German targets all over Europe. There was more to come. Unknown to the Germans, the Allied forces were making secret plans for a massive invasion of Europe on — date as yet unknown — D Day. United States General Dwight D. Eisenhower had been named supreme commander of the operation.

Although the war appeared to be going badly for Hitler, he pressed forward with all his might in his war against the Jews. In fact, he sped things up. Despite all that had been done to annihilate the Jews, the Jews of Hungary were still intact and alive. Almost a million of them.

Again and again, Hitler had urged Hungary, his war partner, to get rid of its Jews. The Hungarian government had passed anti-Semitic laws and stripped Jews of jobs and property. It had put Jews in labor gangs. Hungarian Nazi gangs had routinely beat and murdered Jews. But the government had failed to take the last step — to round up the Jews for deportation. Now, Hungary hesitated for another reason. Hitler's star appeared to be falling. The Hungarian government was uncomfortable about being Hitler's ally.

Hitler lost patience with Hungary and invaded on March 19, 1944. Deportation expert Eichmann came to Hungary and quickly rounded up some Jews for deportation to start the process. Then he threw himself into the task of organizing roundups. And, starting on May 15, four trains, with three thousand Jews in each, left Hungary each day for Auschwitz.

In June, Allied invasion plans were in place. And on June 6, United States and British troops landed in Normandy, France. Attacking on the land, from the sea, and from the air, they began to push Germany out of western Europe. Soviet troops were doing the same in eastern Europe. On July 24, Soviet troops reached, and liberated, the Maidanek death camp. German troops were at last in retreat. The German tanks that had rolled so triumphantly across Europe had been forced to face about and roll back to Germany.

Inside Auschwitz, nothing had changed. Eichmann had deported 437,402 Hungarian Jews — men, women, and children. The trains bringing them arrived daily. On one of the trains was a teenaged boy named Elie Wiesel. He was to survive what he later called "the kingdom of night." In the years that have followed, Wiesel has written and spoken about the horrors he had witnessed. In 1986, he received the Nobel Peace Prize for being "one of the most important spiritual leaders and guides in an age when violence, repression and racism continue to characterize the world."

Despite the war news — and the Soviet advances nearby — the Nazis did not miss a beat in the murder process.

Rather, they redoubled their efforts and tried to kill as many Jews as possible before the Soviets arrived. In order to do so, they kept the gas chambers going day and night. When the ovens could hold no more corpses, they burned the excess in bonfires.

The daily routine of meeting trains from Hungary and making selections was the same. Nor were the Nazis murdering only Hungarian Jews. Trains were still arriving from other points in Europe. In September, among one trainload of Jews from Holland, were Anne Frank and her family — mother, father, and sister Margot. All had been chosen for work.

October was an eventful month. There was a rebellion in Auschwitz. The *Sonderkommando* could no longer face the gruesome task of daily gassings. They knew that eventually, they themselves would be gassed. Rather than wait for that day, they decided to bring on their deaths earlier. They would destroy what they could of the death factory. They could not hope to help the Jews who were arriving each day. But they could slow down the murder process.

Rosa Robota, who worked at the munitions plant, provided the men with explosives. And on October 7, the *Sonderkommando* blew up one crematorium, partly destroyed another, threw their SS overseer into the flames, and killed four others. The Nazis executed the men. And they arrested Rosa Robota and three other women, demanding to know who else was involved. They interrogated and tortured Rosa and her companions for two days. But the young women revealed nothing. The SS hanged them during roll call. Rosa cried from the gallows: "*Chazak ve'ematz*"—"Be strong and have courage!"

It was also an eventful month on the battlefields of eastern

Europe. The Soviets had reached Riga, Latvia, and were gaining ground daily. More defeats for Hitler. There were others as well. Germany was losing the war.

The time had come for the Nazis to cover up the evidence of the "final solution." The Soviets would be in Auschwitz before long. The Nazis had to work fast. Using prisoners as laborers, they dismantled the gas chamber in Birkenau. (The following month, November, they would begin to demolish the crematoria and send the usable parts back to Germany.) They marched thousands of prisoners out into the cold, leading them to other camps or to factories in Germany. Pits containing prisoners' ashes were covered over and planted with grass. Fifty Jewish women prisoners were put to work opening a poorly covered mass grave and burning the corpses.

The trains operated as they had earlier. Those that brought in Jews did not leave empty. Worker prisoners in German concentration camps did not live long. They were either killed or they died of starvation or disease. The SS at Auschwitz continued to receive requests from Germany for worker prisoners. And trains continued to go out with the requested number of slaves. On October 30, several weeks after she arrived, Anne Frank and her sister, Margot, among others, were on a train heading for the Bergen-Belsen concentration camp in Germany. The girls may or may not have known that their mother had been gassed. They may or may not have known that their father was still at Auschwitz.

In January, Warsaw fell to Soviet forces. This meant the Soviets were on the way to Auschwitz. The SS could hear Soviet gunfire. If they delayed, they would be taken prisoner. On January 18, Himmler ordered them to burn the stores containing clothing and supplies. And to evacuate the remaining prisoners to trains for work. The SS set fire to stores and records, and organized the thousands of prisoners for evacuation.

The Nazis lined up the bone-weary, starving men and women prisoners in columns of ten and marched them out into the cold and snow. The prisoners wore only their striped uniforms and shoes, those who still had shoes. They were being marched to trains that would transport them to Germany for work — if they survived the march. Those who fell on the way were shot. Those who turned their heads to see who had been shot were also shot. Those who spoke were beaten. The prisoners marched for days. Few survived the death marches. Out of one column of eight hundred men, some two hundred might arrive at the train alive. The marches were yet another torture, yet another way to kill Jews by natural means. Dr. Aharon Beilin had been at Auschwitz. The shots rang out as he marched with his column through the snow. He later recalled:

> We started counting the shots. It was a long column, five thousand people. Every shot means a human life. Sometimes the shots reached five hundred in a single day.

The Nazis customarily killed sick prisoners. Over eight thousand Jewish prisoners were too sick to walk when the massive evacuation began. There had been no time to kill them all. The Nazis left them behind.

All over Poland — and Germany — the sight was the same, as slave labor camps were being emptied and columns of Jews in striped uniforms were being marched through the snow by the armed SS at their side.

On January 27, 1945, Soviet troops entered and liberated

Auschwitz. In the hospital, among the sick, was Otto Frank, Anne Frank's father. The Soviets found thousands of dazed skeletons in striped rags sitting or wandering about the camp. And pile after pile of corpses. On one of the piles, a figure moved. The person was still alive. It was Wolf Manheimer, the boy who a few years earlier had tried to bicycle to Palestine. He had been a slave laborer. The Nazis had worked him till he fell, given him up for dead, and flung his emaciated body on a pile of corpses.

The Russians were prepared for the sight. They had seen the same sight when they had liberated Maidanek. They also found in Auschwitz records that the Germans had neglected to burn and stores full of human hair, tin cups, eyeglasses, pots and pans, cribs, baby carriages, and such. And also 836,255 women's dresses, 348,000 men's suits, and 38,000 pairs of men's shoes.

In Germany, it was much the same. Allied troops were winning ground and liberating concentration camps. Between April 11 and 28, United States and British troops liberated Buchenwald, Dachau, Bergen-Belsen, and other concentration camps in Germany. The same sights greeted the liberators in all camps — piles of corpses, and dazed skeletons wandering about.

General Dwight D. Eisenhower found some three thousand corpses, buried and unburied, in a camp in Ohrdruf. Because the scene was unimaginable and could not easily be believed, Eisenhower sent pictures to Prime Minister Winston Churchill in London. In a letter to General George C. Marshall he wrote:

> The things I saw beggar description. The visual evidence and the verbal testimony of starvation, cruelty, and bestiality were so overpowering as to leave me a bit sick.

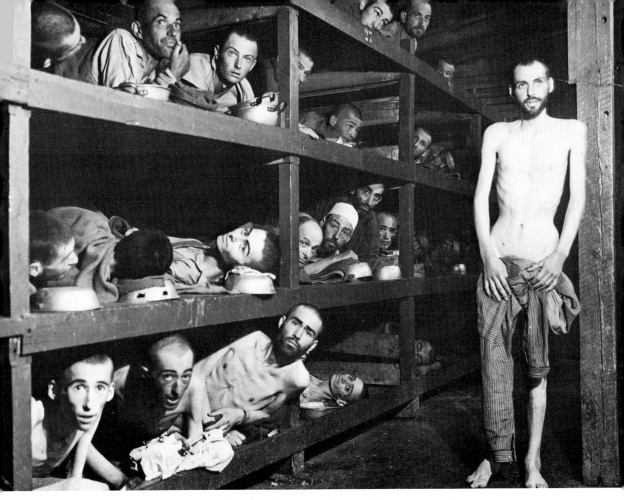

Survivors shown in their bunks at Buchenwald concentration camp, April 16, 1945. *(The Bettmann Archive)*

. . . George Patton would not even enter. He said he would get sick if he did so. I made the visit deliberately, in order to be in a position to give first-hand evidence of these things if ever, in the future, there develops a tendency to charge these allegations merely to "propaganda."

British troops liberated Bergen-Belsen, the camp to which Anne and Margot Frank had been sent. Both had died about two months earlier of typhus. The British liberators found some fifty-eight thousand living skeletons, most of them Jews. Ten thousand unburied corpses lay about the camp. It was learned that the SS had experimented with human skin here, making lamp shades out of it. British Brigadier General H. L. Glyn Hughes, the chief medical officer, also later recorded his impressions in a book.

Anne Frank and tens of thousands of other Jews from all over Europe lay buried in mass graves at Bergen-Belsen. Not far from these graves, the British found a living infant. His name was Menachem Rosensaft and he was born in the camp. His parents had been shipped to Bergen-Belsen from Auschwitz as slave labor. The rest of his family had not been so lucky. His grandparents were murdered at Auschwitz. Also his five-year-old brother. By some miracle, the liberators also found 101 orphaned Jewish children still alive at Bergen-Belsen.

The Allies made the SS in the camps and German civilians from neighboring towns dig graves for the corpses. Jewish inmates helped, and said the prayer for the dead over the graves.

Germany surrendered on May 7, 1945, and on that day the war in Europe was over. A few days before, unable to bear defeat, Hitler had committed suicide in Berlin. So did Himmler. Also Goebbels, after first killing his wife and children. Heydrich had long ago been assassinated in Czechoslovakia.

Before killing himself, Hitler issued a statement to the German people in which he blamed the Jews for starting the war. Nor did he give up his racial beliefs:

> Above all I charge the leaders of this nation and those under them to observe scrupulously the laws of race and

to oppose without mercy the universal poisoner of all peoples, international Jewry.

The Allies arrested Goering, Hoess, and other top Nazis. Eichmann, Dr. Mengele, and many others escaped. They took false names and started new lives in Latin America, the Middle East, the United States, and Canada. A number of them were later found, brought to trial, and punished. Guilty Nazis are still being found today.

Japan surrendered three months later on August 14, ending the war in the Pacific. World War II was finally over.

Hitler had lost the war — and his dream to make Europe German territory. But he nearly succeeded in his aim to destroy the Jews of Europe. Almost the entire Jewish population of Europe — innocent men, women, and children — had disappeared. A handful of Jews remained alive. If World War II had lasted a little longer, Hitler would have had total success.

The survivors of the concentration camps, the emaciated and ragged remnant that was left, stepped out into the world. Those who had survived by living in the woods or by hiding came out into the daylight. Jews who had been living as Christians with false identity cards returned to being Jews.

In Russia, the Jaget family that had lived for two years under a pigpen emerged white-faced, with aching bones and hardly able to walk. In Holland, Mr. and Mrs. Jacobsen came out of the attic after two years and were reunited with their little girl, Ruth.

All over Europe, it was the same. Jews were in a daze. They awoke from their own horror. But they were unaware of what had happened around them. The fate of the Jews of that town, or the next, or of Jews in the other countries was unknown to them. Gradually, they found out.

The surviving Jews were free at last. But free to — what? For the most part, their former countrymen had turned on them. They had no homes to go back to, strangers were living in their homes. They had no families to rejoin. Beside the pain of loss, they suffered a pain they never knew before. Their loved ones had disappeared in flames. They were unable to grieve. They had no grave site to visit, no remains to mourn over. The Jewish family in Europe was no more. The experience of Jack Eisner, the teenager in the Warsaw ghetto whose grandmother had been thrown down the stairs, was typical. He and his mother survived. His grandmother, sister, father, uncles, aunts, and twenty cousins had all disappeared.

S. B. Unsdorfer, a Czech Jew, was at Buchenwald when that camp was liberated. He was still there a few weeks later, when the Jewish holiday of *Shavuot* (Weeks) came about. For the first time in years, he would be able to celebrate a holiday in the open and without fear. An American chaplain was on hand to conduct services. *Shavuot* is an agricultural festival. It also celebrates the time two thousand years ago when the Jews left Egypt and received the Ten Commandments at Mount Sinai. The Bible in Hebrew is called *Torah*, which means "the teaching." Thousands of Jews who had been liberated came to pray. Unsdorfer wrote:

> The cripples, the injured, and the weak came to demonstrate to the world that the last ounce of their strength, the last drop of their blood, and the last breath of their lives belonged to God, to Torah, and to the Jewish religion.
>
> . . . All inmates stood in silence, re-accepting the Torah, whose people, message and purpose Hitler's Germany had attempted to destroy. Jewish history had repeated itself.

Just as our forefathers who were liberated from Egypt accepted the Law in the desert, so did we, the liberated Jews of Buchenwald, re-accept the same Law in the concentration camps of Germany.

The Allies brought relief, medical aid, and food to the prisoners, who now began to be called refugees. The death camps were converted into displaced persons camps. For many Jews, the help came too late. Starvation and disease were too far along, and great numbers died. Jewish organizations also came to help. They tried to give the survivors, especially the children, the feeling that they were not alone, and helped nurse them back to health. They tried to locate the parents or relatives of orphaned children. More often than not, no living relatives could be found.

Jews from Palestine also came to help. A Jewish state would soon be in the making in Palestine. But, for now, Great Britain controlled Palestine. And Britain would not allow more than a handful of homeless Jews to enter Palestine each month, about fifteen hundred. That was not enough. Hundreds of thousands of traumatized Jews were sitting in refugee camps, homeless, with no place to go. The Palestinian Jews took matters into their own hands. They arranged to bring Jews in "illegally," often on old, leaky ships. When the British discovered such a ship, they forced it to turn back to Europe.

When the children at the camps were well enough, they were taken to Palestine. So were the Jewish orphans who had been given away to Christians or churches for safekeeping. Some orphans had grown attached to their foster parents and remained with them. The children in the care of churches and monasteries had been converted to Catholicism. Most

These Jewish survivors protest Britain's efforts to return them to Germany by painting a swastika on the British flag. *(Ruth Gruber)*

returned to Judaism, their original faith. Some did not. One Jewish orphan boy from France remained a Catholic. He is today Cardinal Lustiger of Paris.

There had been no help for the millions of Jews who perished in the flames. The handful that escaped Hitler's inferno had no one to thank except time and the ending of the war. Gradually, they began to leave the camps and build new lives for themselves. The slave-labor survivors had tattooed arms, indelible reminders. Some had the tattoos removed, to erase the past and close off painful questions. Itka Zygmuntowitz kept hers, calling it her "badge of honor." She says, "Let those responsible for it feel ashamed. I am a proud Jewish daughter."

The other survivors, those who had been in hiding, did have someone to thank. They would not have escaped without the help of Christians who fed them, hid them, or helped them on their way. As one survivor said after the war, "All of us are alive today only because somebody saved us."

CHAPTER ELEVEN

The Story of Help

Early in the war, it was possible for Jews to escape from Hitler. Until the end of 1941, the Germans allowed Jews who had visas — official documents to enter another country — to leave. Jewish groups helped fleeing refugees get to Palestine. Quaker groups took Jewish orphans out of Germany and brought them to the United States, England, and Holland.

In the summer of 1939, England all but closed the doors of Palestine to Jewish refugees. Since human lives were at stake, the Jewish underground in Palestine organized their own rescue activities. They bought or rented boats and tried to bring Jews in illegally. Sometimes they succeeded. Most often they did not. The boats were ordered to return to Europe, to Hitler's inferno. Sometimes the boats sank, or were sunk, at sea.

Later, both the United States and England in effect also closed their doors to fleeing Jewish refugees. Once the "final solution" was launched, from the end of 1941 on, the Germans allowed no Jews to leave German-held territory. All hope of escape was gone. The Jews were trapped in Hitler's death net.

The story of help is a strange one. Spain had friendly relations with Germany all during the war. Yet Spain saved over forty thousand Jews by allowing fleeing Jews to enter Spain. Italy fought alongside Germany and was Hitler's partner in the war. Yet Italian officials gave Jewish refugees false identity papers that identified them as Catholics, saving them from Nazi roundups. Italian soldiers helped Jews flee from arriving Germans and did everything possible to keep Jews from falling into German hands. Japan, which also fought on Hitler's side, offered thousands of Jewish refugees sanctuary in the Chinese city of Shanghai, which Japan controlled at the time.

Jews received the least help from their fellow countrymen in countries where anti-Semitism was active even before the war. Poland was such a country. Jews had lived there for over a thousand years. Yet they were regularly attacked, both from church pulpits and by mobs in the street. When Hitler invaded Poland, most Poles added their abuse to that of the Nazis and helped the Nazis round up Jews. Some turned in Jews who were in hiding. Others, however, behaved differently.

There was a death penalty for hiding Jews. Anyone caught doing so was executed. Yet some Poles ran the risk. In Warsaw, some eighteen thousand Jews remained alive after the war because someone had hidden them and fed them out of their own meager rations. Other Poles elsewhere in Poland also saved Jews by hiding them.

Jews understood the perils of help. After the war a Polish Jewish woman who survived those years said she forgave

Poles for not helping Jews because of the danger. But she could never forgive those who informed on Jews.

Russia, a neighbor of Poland, also had a history of anti-Semitism. The Ukraine was the part of Russia that Hitler occupied. Ukrainians were willing helpers of the Nazis in each phase of the death process.

The part France played contributed to the strangeness of the help story. France was a democratic nation and was relatively free of anti-Semitism. Yet when France surrendered to Germany, many French people turned their backs on their Jewish countrymen and even informed on those in hiding.

In other democratic countries, Jews found great humanity. Holland was such a country. As the Germans did in each country they occupied, they also forced Dutch Jews to wear a Jewish star. In Germany, Austria, Poland, and other countries, Jews wearing such badges were taunted, or worse, by the local people. The Dutch responded differently. They called out to Jews wearing stars, "We're with you!" "Wear it with pride." "Good luck!" "We're proud of you." An active Dutch underground helped save many Jews. The Dutch people as a whole, like the Italian people as a whole, helped protect and hide their Jewish fellow countrymen.

In Amsterdam, Anne Frank and her family hid for two years with the help of Christian friends. But even Holland had its informers. The Germans came to the annex where the Frank family and other Jews were hiding and put them on trains. Except for the father, the entire family died at the hands of the Nazis. The informer received $1.40 as a reward.

In Belgium and elsewhere in Europe, many Christians hid Jewish children.

How did governments respond to the plight of the Jews? The response was different from country to country. France fought against Germany. Then Hitler invaded France and occupied most of the country. In the part of France that Germany did not occupy, French people formed a new government in the city of Vichy. The section was called Vichy France. Vichy supported Nazi principles and was pro-German. It made laws against the Jews and rounded up a quarter of the Jewish population of France for "deportation." It went even further. To earn the favor of the Germans, it voluntarily rounded up four thousand Jewish orphans between the ages of two and twelve. Many of the children could have been saved. There were people who would have hidden them. But the Vichy people refused to listen to such pleas and put the frightened children on trains bound for Auschwitz. The children met the expected fate; they were murdered on arrival.

Arab nations were hostile to Jews. Yet King Muhammed V of Morocco protected some 300,000 Moroccan Jews from the pro-Nazi Vichy government in France that controlled his country.

In the Scandinavian countries, government and people acted as one. When the Germans occupied Denmark, they introduced the usual anti-Jewish laws. Danish Christians publicly opposed the laws. A Dane who repeated the German anti-Semitic slogans was tried in a Danish court. When the Germans demanded that the Jews be rounded up for "deportation," King Christian X refused. Later, Germany decided to bypass the king and round up the Jews in a surprise attack. A German civilian working in Denmark learned of the plan and told Danish officials. The officials told Rabbi Marcus Melchior, the head of the Jewish community. The holiday of Rosh HaShanah, the Jewish New Year, was about to begin. In soft tones, the rabbis so informed the Jews who gathered at the synagogue for prayer. They hurried out to call everyone they knew, and the news spread quickly. The Danish people hid the Jews in their homes, hospitals, and elsewhere.

Neighboring Sweden also came to the rescue. Under cover of night, the entire Jewish population of Denmark — some seven thousand men, women, and children — were ferried across the water in fishing boats to safety in Sweden. When the Germans struck in Denmark, they were surprised. They came with their lists of Jewish names and addresses. But they found the synagogue empty and no one at home at the Jewish addresses.

Finland reacted in a similar way. When the Germans told the foreign minister of Finland to round up the Jews, he answered, "We prefer to die with the Jews; we shall never betray them."

Government help also came from two unexpected sources. Bulgaria fought on Germany's side during the war. But when Hitler demanded that Bulgaria round up its Jews, King Boris made one excuse after the other, delaying and saving the Jews of Bulgaria.

Romania was another unexpected source of help. Early in the war, when Hitler was winning, the brutal Iron Guard of Romania massacred the Jews of Bucharest, the capital. They photographed the bodies they had mutilated, to have souvenirs. Later, when the Nazis ordered the remaining Jews to be "deported" to Belzec, the Romanian government refused. Germany was losing the war by then.

And individual voices? Were there no ministers or public officials to cry out against Nazi policies? Very few. In Germany, around the time of the *Kristallnacht* episode, Father Bernard Lichtenberg of Berlin was arrested for speaking out against Nazi policies and holding public prayers for the Jews.

The Catholic priest died on the way to a concentration camp. Also in Germany, a small group of students calling itself the White Rose distributed leaflets to the public to protest Nazi policy. The Nazis executed the young men and women leaders of the group by beheading them.

Around the same time, Pastor J. von Jan in Swabia told his congregation:

> Men who have locally served our nation and conscientiously done their duty, have been thrown into concentration camps simply because they belong to a different race. Our nation's infamy is bound to bring about Divine punishment.

Nazi mobs dragged Pastor Jan from his vicarage, beat him, and smashed the vicarage. The pastor was imprisoned.

Oscar Schindler was a German who owned a factory in Cracow, Poland. He made products needed by the German army. He saved many Jews from death as a matter of policy by asking for them to work in his factory, saying he needed them to help the German war effort.

When the French Jews were being rounded up for deportation, Marc Boegner, a French Protestant minister, pleaded with the Vichy government to spare the four thousand children and not to send them to Auschwitz. His pleas went unanswered. But his continuing protests, and those of other prominent Protestants in Vichy, helped save the rest of the Jews of France.

Official documents were also lifesavers. A visa is official permission to enter a country. Having one in the early days of the war meant the difference between life and death. Sempo Sugihara was a Japanese diplomat in Lithuania, a country then under German control. The Lithuanian Jews were in mortal danger. Sugihara wired Japan, asking for permission to extend visas to them. When he received no answer and because there was no more time to wait, Sugihara, his wife, and his staff issued some six thousand visas and identity cards to the Jews, hand writing many of them, to hasten the process. As the Jews came to take the visas, Sugihara taught them to say in Japanese *"Banzai Nippon,"* "Long live Japan," so they could say at least those few words.

A passport from a neutral country also made the difference between life and death. A passport is a stamp of citizenship. It says the passport holder is a citizen of that country. Under international law, Germany was forced to honor the passports of neutral countries.

Raoul Wallenberg, a Swedish diplomat in Hungary, was on a rescue mission in that country. After the Eichmann deportations, some two hundred thousand Jews were still alive in Hungary. Wallenberg did all he could to save them. Eichmann and the Nazis strove mightily to deport the remaining Jews. With financial help from the United States–created War Refugee Board, Wallenberg strove just as mightily to outwit the Nazis. He bought buildings and flew the Swedish flag over them, making the buildings Swedish territory. Persons living in such houses were under the protection of Sweden. Hundreds of Jews crowded into the protected houses for safety. They were not always safe. The Arrow Cross was a murderous Hungarian Nazi group. Gangs seized Jews from the houses and took them to the Danube River. Sometimes they shot them and left them. Sometimes they tied them in groups of three and shot the middle person, killing one and causing the two who fell with him to drown.

Wallenberg also created a special Swedish protective pass-

Raoul Wallenberg strove to save the Hungarian Jews. *(Raoul Wallenberg Committee of the United States)*

port. The Jews who received these passports were able to leave Hungary and escape Eichmann's roundups. Some diplomats from other neutral countries (the papal nuncio, Swiss, Portuguese, and Spanish representatives) followed Wallenberg's lead and did the same, saving yet other lives. A priest in Turkey, Angelo Roncalli, issued fake baptismal certificates in 1944 to Hungarians, to save them from the Nazis. In 1958, Father Roncalli became Pope John XXIII. A Jewish organization printed additional copies of the certificate and yet other Jews were saved.

Wallenberg did everything humanly possible, frustrating the Nazis wherever he could. Despite his tireless efforts, he was able to save only half the Hungarian Jews. The Gestapo had tried several times to assassinate him, without success. But Wallenberg met a mysterious end. He disappeared. After Russian forces liberated Hungary from the Germans, he was seen going into Soviet headquarters in Budapest and was never seen or heard from again.

The Jews tell a story: God is not pleased with the way people have turned out. They are selfish, greedy, and mean spirited. But, in each generation, there are thirty-six good and noble souls. People who are saints. And for their sake, because of their goodness, God allows the world to continue to exist.

Jews call these good souls *lamed vav-niks*. The nickname is made of two Hebrew letters that stand for the numbers 30 and 6. Jews believe that in times of trouble, a *lamed vav-nik* appears almost from out of nowhere to help them. The person may be anyone, a beggar or someone well born.

The Jews are the oldest continuous civilization in the Western world. The ancient Greeks and Romans have disappeared, but the Jews are still here. They have been persecuted for some two thousand years. In times of need, they have fought back or moved out of harm's way. They believe they have been saved by a few things: Their love of God. By celebrating their holidays and maintaining their traditions. And by the *lamed vav-niks* who have come to their rescue in times of trouble. For many Jews, Raoul Wallenberg is a *lamed vav-nik*.

CHAPTER TWELVE

After the War

Considering the scope of their crimes, the Nazis succeeded fairly well in keeping the "final solution" secret. They had the help of the chaos of wartime, which is a natural cover-up. The code words they used also covered their deeds. Of considerable help was the unbelievable nature of the acts. Throughout the war, reports filtered out into the free world in bits and pieces. Many heads of state found it difficult to believe the reports and tended to discount them. Sir Winston Churchill, the British prime minister, accepted them at face value. He declared in November 1941:

> None has suffered more cruelly than the Jew the unspeakable evils wrought on the bodies and spirits of men by Hitler and his vile regime. The Jew bore the brunt of the Nazis' first onslaught upon the citadels of freedom and human dignity.

And later, in July 1944, when the "final solution" was on the way to becoming a reality, Churchill wrote to a member

This sculpture at Yad Vashem in Jerusalem is a memorial to the six million. *(James Casson/Art Resource, NY)*

of his cabinet, "There is no doubt that this is probably the greatest and most horrible single crime ever committed in the whole history of the world."

After the war, all heads of state, and the general public as well, learned of the "final solution." From journalists, war trials, and new words that were brought into use, the gruesome details — and the scope of the nightmare — gradually unfolded.

War, by its nature, means killing and destruction. But Nazi barbarism exceeded anything that was known in the modern world. There were no words with which to speak of evil on such a scale. The word that was brought into use to speak of it was *Holocaust*. It comes from the Greek and means "destruction of an entirety, a whole." The word *genocide* came into use to mean "murder of a segment of the world's population." And a new category of crime was created — crimes against humanity.

The United States, Great Britain, the Soviet Union, and France brought the leading Nazis to trial, charging them with crimes against humanity. Fittingly, the trials were held in Nuremberg, the city in which Hitler passed laws to legalize hatred and irrationality. Witness after witness appeared to testify — survivors themselves, officers of the Allied armies, people from all over Europe, non-Nazi Germans, even some Nazis. Emmanuel Ringelblum's diaries were found, also the diaries of others. Blueprints of the destroyed gas chambers were found, and many secret German documents. From these various sources, the grim details of the "final solution" became known.

Goering was found guilty at the trial in Nuremberg. He killed himself to escape punishment. Hoess bragged at the trial, "We executed about 400,000 Hungarian Jews alone." Found guilty, he was hanged on the gallows that once stood near the kitchen at Auschwitz. General Stroop, who had set the Warsaw ghetto on fire, was hanged in Warsaw. Eichmann had escaped for the time being. He was in hiding in Argentina. But he would be found in due course.

Supreme Court Justice Robert Jackson, representing the United States at the Nuremberg trials, said to the court:

> The wrongs we seek to condemn and punish have been so calculated, so malignant and so devastating, that civilization cannot tolerate their being ignored because it cannot survive their being repeated.

The trials at Nuremberg were not the only trials that took place. Others would take place in other countries as well.

Trials are still taking place today.

The lives that were lost in Hitler's inferno could not be brought back to life. But some wounds were healed after the war.

The Catholic church withdrew the teaching that Jews of all centuries were to be held responsible for the death of Jesus. In December 1986, speaking in Sydney, Australia, Pope John Paul II said:

> Where Catholics are concerned, it will continue to be an explicit and very important part of my mission to repeat and emphasize that our attitude to the Jewish religion should be one of the greatest respect, since the Catholic faith is rooted in the eternal truths contained in the Hebrew scriptures, and in the irrevocable Covenant made with Abraham.

Major Lutheran bodies have also taken new positions. The Fourth Lutheran World Federation Consultation on the Church and the Jewish people met in Geneva, Switzerland, on September 8, 1982. On that occasion, they issued a statement to all member Lutheran churches throughout the world declaring,

> We Christians today must purge ourselves of any hatred of the Jews and any sort of teaching of contempt for Judaism.

German heads of state continue to remind Germans to remember their Nazi past. West German Chancellor Helmut Kohl said in Bonn on January 20, 1987:

> The memory of those who were deported in Germany's name, enslaved, humiliated and murdered in the extermi-

nation camps of Auschwitz, Treblinka, Birkenau, Maidanek and Sobibor obliges us never again to stir feelings of hatred.

The greatest healing came from the creation of a Jewish state. This idea had been in the making since after World War I, when the League of Nations gave Great Britain control over Palestine until a Jewish homeland could be established. Both Jews and Arabs lived there. Great Britain divided Palestine, establishing present-day Jordan in the larger part, and a Jewish homeland in the smaller. But the Jewish homeland failed to develop because of Arab opposition. After World War II, the United Nations divided what remained of Palestine between Jews and Arabs, making a homeland for each.

On May 14, 1948, the Jews proclaimed the existence of a Jewish state. They called it Israel — after the patriarch Jacob whose name the wrestling angel had changed to Israel. The Arabs were unwilling to accept the existence of a Jewish state, and armies of neighboring Arab states attacked. Israel fought a war of independence and won. Almost two thousand years after Rome had destroyed Jerusalem, the Jews were once more a free nation in their ancestral home.

Many Jews were already living in Palestine. Now, after the creation of the state, other Jews began to return in droves.

It was the new government of Israel that found Adolf Eichmann living under a false name in Argentina, brought him to Jerusalem for a public trial, and executed him for his crimes against humanity.

In Hebrew, the Holocaust is called *Shoa*. The word appears three times in the Bible, referring each time to a place that had been brought to waste and ruin by a great upheaval.

In May of 1949, Israel became a member of the United Nations.
Here, Israeli officials participate in the flag-raising ceremony at
UN headquarters. *(United Nations)*

As a way to remember the upheaval, the Israeli Parliament created the holiday of *Yom HaShoa* — Day of the Shoa. It is celebrated on the twenty-seventh day of the Hebrew month of Nisan, some time in late March or early April.

The Parliament also established a permanent monument to those who perished: *Yad Vashem* — Memorial and Record. It is located on Mount Remembrance in Jerusalem. The monument is a gracious park dotted with statues and symbols. One is a building called Remembrance Hall. On its mosaic floor are the names of the largest concentration camps. An eternal flame burns near them. United States Secretary of State George P. Shultz, on a visit to Yad Vashem, said it was a reminder that "mankind's capacity for evil is unbounded."

There are also monuments to courage and goodness at Yad Yashem. A statue of Dr. Korczak and the orphans is dedicated to the memory of the million Jewish children who were destroyed in the Holocaust. Avenue of Righteous Gentiles is a tree-lined walk. Each tree has been planted in the name of a Christian who risked his or her life to save Jews. New acts of heroism are discovered all the time, and trees continue to be planted to this day.

The Nazis believed that the Germany Hitler had created would last for a thousand years. Fortunately for the world, Hitler's Germany lasted only twelve years. Before the war, there were forty-five hundred Jewish communities in some twenty countries, all active, vibrant centers of Jewish learning and thought. Hitler erased those communities from the map of the world. Six million Jews disappeared.

The figure has become a symbol of the nightmare. Like all symbols, its function is limited. It resonates an event, but it cannot describe. It fails to convey the bestiality of the Nazis

Inside Remembrance Hall at Yad Vashem, Israel.

and the suffering of their victims. And — because so large a figure cannot be grasped — it also fails to convey both the number of Jews who were wantonly murdered and the fact that they were people. Six million. Behind each digit, starting with the number one, was a pair of eyes, a face, a living, vital human being.

Some Jews who survived the war lost their faith in God. They say God abandoned them and ask, "Where was God?" Others feel differently. They say the question to ask is "Where was man?" Human evil is man's responsibility, not God's.

They are united in another thought. In Italy, in the former Jewish ghetto of Venice, is a monument cast by the artist Arbit Blatas and inscribed in English, French, and Italian with a poem by the former mayor of Venice, André Tronc. The monument appears also at United Nations' Dag Hammerskjöld Plaza in New York, Paris, and other cities. The final words of the poem speak for all Jews:

> Your sad holocaust is engraved in History,
> And nothing shall purge your deaths
> from our memories.
> For our memories are your only grave.

The memorial by Arbit Blatas at the Dag Hammerskjöld Plaza in New York. (*International Center for Holocaust Studies of the Anti-Defamation League of B'nai B'rith*)

Some Books About the Holocaust

Background and Documents

Baynes, N. H., ed. *The Speeches of Adolf Hitler.* New York: Fertig, 1969.

Cohn, Norman. *Warrant for Genocide: The Myth of the Jewish World Conspiracy and the Protocols of the Elders of Zion.* New York: Harper & Row, 1967.

Dawidowicz, Lucy S., ed. *A Holocaust Reader.* New York: Behrman House, 1976. The editor traces the development of the Holocaust and the "final solution" through key Nazi and Jewish documents of the period — memos, letters, speeches, reports, and other such materials.

Documents of the Holocaust. Jerusalem: Yad Vashem, 1981. Nazi Party memos, excerpts from Goebbels's diary, *Mein Kampf, Einsatzgruppen* and SS reports on *Aktions,* roundups, etc., copies of the Nuremberg Laws, lists of valuables and personal belongings sent from death camps to Nazi headquarters, and other documents and records.

Encyclopedia Judaica. "Anti-Semitism."

———. "Badges." About the articles of clothing Jews were forced to wear to identify themselves over the ages.

Gilbert, Martin, ed. *Atlas of the Holocaust.* London: Michael Joseph, 1982.

Hitler, Adolf. *Mein Kampf.* Boston: Houghton Mifflin, 1943.

Lanzmann, Claude. *Shoah, An Oral History of the Holocaust.* New York: Pantheon Books, 1985. Transcript of a film in which the author interviews Jews and Christians who witnessed the events of the Holocaust.

Mosse, George L. *Nazi Culture: A Documentary History.* New York: Schocken Books, 1981. Printed documents reflecting Nazi thinking, with author's comments.

History

Dawidowicz, Lucy S. *The War Against the Jews 1933–1945.* New York: Holt, Rinehart & Winston, 1975.

Gilbert, Martin. *The Holocaust, A History of the Jews of Europe During the Second World War.* New York: Holt, Rinehart & Winston, 1985. The stories of Dr. Aharon Beilin, Hugo Gryn, and those of many others, appear more fully in this work.

Hilberg, Raul. *The Destruction of the European Jews.* New York: Holmes & Meier, 1985. Three volumes. Also a greatly condensed paper edition for students.

Levin, Nora. *The Holocaust: The Destruction of European Jewry 1933–1945.* New York: Schocken Books, 1973.

Shirer, William L. *The Rise and Fall of the Third Reich: A History of Nazi Germany.* New York: Simon & Schuster, 1960.

For Young Readers

Abells, Chana Byers. *The Children We Remember.* Rockville, Md.: Kar-Ben Copies, 1983; New York: Greenwillow Books, 1987. Photographs of children and short captions.

Altshuler, David A. *Hitler's War Against the Jews*. New York: Behrman House, 1978. An adaptation of *The War Against the Jews* by Lucy S. Dawidowicz.

Katz, William Loren. *An Album of Nazism*. New York: Franklin Watts, 1979. A short history in pictures and captions.

Meltzer, Milton. *Never to Forget: The Jews of the Holocaust*. New York: Harper & Row, 1976.

Anthologies

Friedlander, Albert H., ed. *A Reader of Holocaust Literature*. New York: Schocken Books, 1976.

Glatstein, Jacob, and others, eds. *Anthology of Holocaust Literature*. New York: Atheneum, 1980. The stories of Shaye Gertner, S. B. Unsdorfer, and others are included.

Rothchild, Sylvia, ed. *Voices from the Holocaust*. New York: New American Library, 1982. The stories of Dr. William Glicksman and others are included.

Individual Accounts

Des Pres, Terence. *The Survivor: An Anatomy of Life in the Death Camps*. New York: Oxford University Press, 1976.

Donat, Alexander. *The Holocaust Kingdom: A Memoir*. New York: Holt, Rinehart & Winston, 1967. His experiences in the Warsaw ghetto.

Eisner, Jack. *The Survivor*. New York: Morrow, 1980.

Flender, Harold. *Rescue in Denmark*. New York: Simon & Schuster, 1963.

Hart, Kitty. *Return to Auschwitz*. New York: Atheneum, 1985.

Lester, Elenore. *Wallenberg; The Man in the Iron Web*. Englewood Cliffs, N.J.: Prentice-Hall, 1982.

Meed, Vladka. *On Both Sides of the Wall*. New York: Holocaust Library, 1979. Her experiences as a courier and in the underground.

Tec, Nechama. *Dry Tears: The Story of a Lost Childhood.* New York: Oxford University Press, 1984. How she survived the war by passing as a Christian in Poland.

Wells, Leon. *The Death Brigade.* New York: Holocaust Library, 1978. About his escape from a concentration camp and recapture by the Nazis.

Wiesel, Elie. *Night.* New York: Hill & Wang, 1960. A classic memoir about his experiences in concentration camps.

For Young Readers

Atkinson, Lynda. *In Kindling Flame: The Story of Hannah Senesh 1921–1944* New York: Lothrop, Lee & Shepard Books, 1985. A young Jewish girl tries to rescue Jews in Hungary, is caught by the Nazis and executed.

Flinker, Moshe. *Young Moshe's Diary: The Spiritual Torment of a Jewish Boy in Nazi Europe.* Edited by Saul Esh and Geoffrey Wigoder, Jerusalem: Yad Vashem, 1965.

Gershon, Karen. *We Came as Children: A Collective Autobiography.* New York: Harcourt, Brace & World, 1966.

Hersh, Gizelle, and Peggy Mann. *Gizelle, Save the Children!* New York: Dodd, Mead, 1980. A young girl's experiences in Auschwitz.

Reiss, Johanna. *The Upstairs Room.* New York: Thomas Y. Crowell, 1972. Two Dutch Jewish girls are hidden, and saved, by a Christian family.

Suhl, Yuri. *Uncle Misha's Partisans.* New York: Four Winds Press, 1973. About Jewish partisans in the woods fighting the Nazis.

Tridenti, Lina. *Anne Frank.* Morristown, N.J.: Silver Burdett, 1985. Translated from the Italian by Stephen Thorne.

Diaries

Hoess, Rudolf. *Commandant of Auschwitz: The Autobiography of Rudolf Hoess.* Cleveland: World Publishing, 1959.

Kaplan, Chaim A. *The Warsaw Diary of Chaim A. Kaplan*. Edited and translated by Abraham I. Katsch, New York: Collier Books, 1973.

Korczak, Janusz. *Ghetto Diary*. New York: Holocaust Library, 1978.

Ringelblum, Emmanuel. *Notes from the Warsaw Ghetto*. Edited and translated by Jacob Sloan, New York: McGraw-Hill, 1958.

Song Books

Kalisch, Shoshana, and Barbara Meister, eds. *Yes, We Sang! Songs of the Ghettos and Concentration Camps*. New York: Harper & Row, 1985. Songs, history, biographies.

Mlotek, Eleanor, and Malke Gottlieb, eds. *We are Here: Songs of the Holocaust*. New York: Workmen's Circle, 1983. Translated by Roslyn Bresnick Perry.

About the Trials

Gilbert, G. M. *Nuremberg Diary*. New York: Farrar, Straus & Cudahy, 1947.

Hausner, Gideon. *Justice in Jerusalem*. New York: Schocken Books, 1968. About the Eichmann trial.

Kitner, E. W., ed. *The Hadamar Trial*. London: William Hodge, 1949.

Neave, Airey. *On Trial at Nuremberg*. New York: Little, Brown, 1979.

Archives

Video Archive for Holocaust Testimonies at Yale, Sterling Memorial Library, Room 331C, New Haven, Conn.

YIVO, an institute for Jewish research, 1048 Fifth Avenue, New York, N.Y.

Yad Vashem, The Holocaust Martyrs and Heroes Remembrance Authority, Jerusalem.

The following accounts, cited briefly in the book, appear more fully in the following source:

Wolf Manheimer and Menachem Z. Rosensaft, in vol. 30, no. 5, of *Keeping Posted*, the monthly magazine of the Union of American Hebrew Congregations.

The accounts of Annette Baslaw, Jack Jaget, Ruth Jacobsen, and Itka Zygmuntowicz were told to the author by the individuals. Accounts of unnamed people are from an eye witness or someone who heard the story from an eye witness.

Index

Page numbers in *italics* refer to pages with illustrations.

Nuremberg war crimes trials, 131-32

Ohrdruf death camp, 112
"Operation Blot-Out," 85

Palestine, 12, 34, 117, 120,
    133. *See also* Israel
Passover, 13, 77
Patton, George, 113
Pearl Harbor, 65
Pharisees, 9
Poland, 37, 39, 41-43, *43*, 45,
    47-48, 65-66, 81
    German invasion of Poland,
        41, 121
    See also Warsaw ghetto
Pontius Pilate, 11, 12
Protestants, 17-18
*Protocols of the Wise Men—or
    Elders—of Zion*, 21-22,
    23

Quakers, 120

Rabbis, 9
Rabbi's Speech, The (Retcliffe),
    20
Retcliffe, Sir John, 20
Ringelblum, Emmanuel, 62-
    64, 73, 79, 131
Robota, Rosa, 109
Roman Catholic Church, 13,
    17, 132

Romania, 124
Romans, 8-9, 10-11, 12
Roncalli, Angelo, 127
Rosensaft, Menachem, 114
Russia. *See* Soviet Union
Russian Revolution, 22

SA. *See* Storm troops (SA)
Sabbath, 13, 14
Sadducees, 9
Sarah, 7-8
Schindler, Oscar, 125
Schutzstaffel. See SS
    (Schutzstaffel)
SD (German intelligence unit),
    29
Semites, 7
Shabbesdikkeh, 56
Shavuot, 116
Shem, 7
Shoa, 133-135
Shultz, Secretary of State
    George P., 135
Slave labor. *See* Labor camps
Sobibor death camp, 81
Solomon, King, 8
Sonderkommando, 96, 97, 109
Soviet Union, 60, 122
    anti-Semitism in, 21-22
    war crimes trials, 131
Spain, 121
Speer, Albert, 25
SS *(Schutzstaffel)*, 28-29, 31,
    38, 45, 47-48, 51, 65-66,
    72, 77, 91, 97